Introducing
International
Social Work

Introducing International Social Work

EDITED BY

**Sue Lawrence, Karen Lyons,
Graeme Simpson and
Nathalie Huegler**

Series Editors: Jonathan Parker and Greta Bradley

LearningMatters

First published in 2009 by Learning Matters Ltd.

British Library Cataloguing in Publication Data
A CIP record for this book is available from the British Library.

ISBN: 978 1 84445 132 6

Cover and text design by Code 5 Design Associates Ltd
Project Management by Deer Park Productions, Tavistock
Typeset by Pantek Arts Ltd, Maidstone, Kent
Printed and bound in Great Britain by Bell & Bain Ltd, Glasgow

Learning Matters Ltd
33 Southernhay East
Exeter EX1 1NX
Tel: 01392 215560
info@learningmatters.co.uk
www.learningmatters.co.uk

Mixed Sources
Product group from well-managed forests and other controlled sources
www.fsc.org   Cert no. TT-COC-002769
© 1996 Forest Stewardship Council

FSC

Contents

vi

Acknowledgements

The editors and authors appreciated the support of the International sub-committee of the Joint University Council Social Work Education Committee (JUC SWEC) in initiating this project and the financial assistance received from JUC SWEC and SWAP for its development.

Editors and contributors

Jane Foggin qualified as a social worker at Nottingham University in 1992, where she completed her Masters dissertation on feminist approaches to women's groups in a statutory social work setting. She worked for some years as an Approved Social Worker in community mental health services. She moved to a role as a training and development specialist in mental health, working for Nottinghamshire County Council in this role for five years. She is now employed as a Senior Lecturer at Sheffield Hallam University, in the Social Work, Social Care and Community Studies subject group. She is the course leader for the BA (Hons) Social Work, and specialises in teaching about social perspectives in mental health, and social work professional processes of assessment, planning, intervention and review. She is currently researching issues regarding employability and students' perceptions of the linkage between their current studies and subsequent employment.

Nathalie Huegler trained as a social worker in Germany and has since worked with young refugees in different settings, currently as a senior social worker supporting child torture survivors for a charity in London. After completing an MA in International Social Work and Refugee Studies at the University of East London (in 2004), she is now studying towards a PhD at London Metropolitan University, focusing on social work with separated children, and human rights, from a crossnational comparative perspective. Other activities include editorial assistance work for the journal *International Social Work*, and part-time teaching at London Metropolitan University.

Marelize Joubert trained as a social worker in South Africa and has since worked with children and young people and vulnerable adults in a variety of different settings, currently as a senior lecturer in the subject group of Social Work, Social Care and Communities Studies at Sheffield Hallam University. She teaches on the Inter-professional strand of the Faculty and has an interest in dual diagnoses, substance misuse and mental health. Marelize is also the Course Leader for the Masters in Social Work, a postgraduate qualifying course. She has undertaken research into the effectiveness of aftercare services for service users experiencing substance misuse problems as well as consultancy work alongside the Nursing Subject Group on addiction studies for local Primary Care Trusts and NHS. Marelize is currently completing a Masters in Public Sector Management via the University of Westminster.

Sue Lawrence qualified as a social worker in 1976 and has been a social work educator since 1991, currently Principal Lecturer in International Social Work at London Metropolitan University. Sue has been actively involved in European social work research, networks and exchanges throughout her career and is a Course Director of the MA Comparative European Social Studies (MACESS) and Course Leader of the Professional Doctorate International Social Work. Sue is currently UK representative on the European Association of Schools of Social Work (EASSW), is on the editorial board of the *European Journal of Social Work* and is a reviewer for the journal *International Social Work*.

Brian Littlechild is Professor of Social Work and Associate Head of the School of Health and Social, Community and Health Studies, University of Hertfordshire. A qualified and registered social worker, he specialised in work with children, young people and their families, and people with mental health problems before working in universities. He has researched and published widely on violence against staff, young offenders, child protection, mental health and risk assessment. A Board member of the International Association of Schools of Social Work, and its Publications Editor, he is also a founding Board member of the European Research Institute of Social Work, University of Ostrava, Czech Republic, and Organising Tutor, *Social Work Theories and Methodologies programme*, Inter University Centre, Dubrovnik.

Karen Lyons began her career in school social work, then taught social work for 26 years at the University of East London. She initiated a degree year option in International Social Work in the 1990s which was subsequently developed into an MA programme. These courses drew on experience gained through an ERASMUS network, including student exchange programmes. She is now an Emeritus Professor (International Social Work) at London Metropolitan University where she is based as the editor-in-chief of the Journal, *International Social Work*. Other current work includes research student supervision; writing; and consultancy work, in the UK and abroad.

Vicky Price spent ten years in social work practice before beginning her career in social work education in 1986, subsequently joining the University of Wolverhampton, where she is now Principal Lecturer for social work, social care and social policy. She has a long-standing interest in learning disability and has developed links with organisations in Amsterdam, where she also teaches on an ERASMUS exchange. She has organised placements for overseas students in the UK, and has led and contributed to international seminars in Brussels and London.

Graeme Simpson spent 19 years in child care social work before joining the University of Wolverhampton in 1997, where he has organised successful overseas student placements. European and international social work is a specialist interest and he has led international seminars in Belgium, Germany and the Netherlands as well as in the UK. A current focus of his work is developing the international perspective within mainstream social work education. Other work includes being a member of the Book Review Panel for *European Journal of Social Work* and reviewing papers for *International Social Work*.

Janet E. Williams worked in an experimental mental health project before joining Sheffield Hallam University in 1990. As a Principal Lecturer she has responsibility for developing and co-ordinating international activities including international student placements, curriculum development and staff exchanges. Recently she led an EU-funded Curriculum Development Project (SWIPE) with five other European universities, to write an international module. Her international curriculum developmental work has extended to Hong Kong and post-Soviet countries (EU Tempus Project). Janet has also published in the field of mental health. She is currently the UK representative on the International Association of Schools of Social Work (IASSW).

Introduction

Sue Lawrence and Karen Lyons

If you are just beginning a social work course, or you are thinking about becoming a social worker, you may be wondering why you need to consider international social work. Alternatively, you might have an interest in working in another country and have started reading this book for information that might help you achieve that goal; you may have thought about the diverse nature of our population and wondered if looking beyond this country's boundaries might help you understand more about our society; or you may be curious about the nature of social problems and social work in other countries and want to learn how other societies approach social issues. All of these points are relevant to studying international social work. Indeed, our aim in writing this book is to locate social work as an increasingly international profession and to explore some of the international issues and activities that social workers are engaged with in their daily practice. To do this, we draw on practice examples, projects and research from here in the UK as well as using examples from other countries to illustrate some of the ways in which social issues are perceived and tackled in both our own and in different societies.

We have therefore written this book for student social workers who are beginning to develop their skills and understanding of the requirements for practice and have a curiosity and interest in the international dimensions of social work. While it is primarily aimed at students in their first year or level of study, it will be useful for subsequent years, depending on how your programme is designed, what you are studying and especially as you move into practice learning. The book will also appeal to people considering a career in social work or social care but not yet studying for a social work degree. It will assist students undertaking a range of social and health care courses in further education. Nurses, occupational therapists and other health and social care professionals will be able to gain an insight into the new requirements demanded of social workers. Experienced and qualified social workers, especially those contributing to practice learning, will also be able to use this book for consultation, teaching, revision and to gain an insight into the expectations raised within the qualifying degree in social work.

Requirements for social work education

Social work education in the UK has undergone a major transformation to ensure that qualified social workers are educated to honours degree level and develop knowledge, skills and values which are common and shared. A vision for social work operating in complex human situations has been adopted. This is reflected in the following definition from the International Association of Schools of Social Work (IASSW) and International Federation of Social Workers (IFSW).

The social work profession promotes social change, problem solving in human relationships and the empowerment and liberation of people to enhance well-being.

Utilising theories of human behaviour and social systems, social work intervenes at the points where people interact with their environments. Principles of human rights and social justice are fundamental to social work.

(IFSW, 2000)

While there is a great deal packed into this short definition it encapsulates the notion that social work concerns individual people and wider society. Social workers practise with people who are vulnerable, who are struggling in some way to participate fully in society. Social workers walk that tightrope between the marginalised individual and the social and political environment that may have contributed to their marginalisation.

Social workers need to be highly skilled and knowledgeable to work effectively in this context. In order to improve the quality of professional social work, it is crucial that you, as a student social worker, develop a rigorous grounding in and understanding of theories and models for social work. Such knowledge helps social workers to know what to do, when to do it and how to do it, while recognising that social work is a complex activity with no absolute 'rights' and 'wrongs' of practice for each situation.

Learning features

The book is interactive. You are encouraged to work through it as an active participant, taking responsibility for your learning in order to increase your knowledge, understanding and ability to apply this learning to practice. You are expected to reflect creatively on how immediate learning needs can be met in gaining an international perspective on social work and how your professional learning can be developed in your future career.

Case studies throughout the book help you to examine theories and models for social work practice. We have devised activities that require you to reflect on experiences, situations and events and help you to review and summarise learning undertaken. In this way your knowledge becomes deeply embedded as part of your development. When you come to practice learning in an agency, the work and reflection undertaken here will help you to improve and hone your skills and knowledge.

This book introduces knowledge and learning activities for you as a student social worker concerning the central processes relating to issues of daily practice in all areas of the discipline. Suggestions for further reading are made at the end of each chapter.

Professional development and reflective practice

Great emphasis is placed on developing skills of reflection about, in and on practice. This has developed over many years in social work. It is important also that you reflect prior to practice, if indeed this is your goal. This book assists you in developing a questioning approach that looks in a critical way at your thoughts, experiences and practice and seeks to heighten your skills in refining your practice as a result of these deliberations. Reflection is central to good social work practice, but only if action results from that reflection.

Reflecting about, in and on your practice is not only important during your education to become a social worker; it is considered key to continuing professional development. As we move to a profession that acknowledges lifelong learning as a way of keeping up to date, ensuring that research informs practice, and that acknowledges the necessity of honing skills and values for practice, it is important to begin the process at the outset of your development. The importance of professional development is clearly shown by its inclusion in the National Occupational Standards and it is reflected in the General Social Care Council (GSCC) Code of Practice for Employees.

The Quality Assurance Agency for Higher Education (QAA) has developed subject benchmark statements that provide general standards of attributes and capabilities expected of those receiving qualifications at a given level for specific subject areas. In this book we outline the relevant subject benchmarks for social work (QAA, 2008) at the beginning of each chapter so you can clearly chart your progress in meeting these standards.

The structure of this book

The book concentrates on models that are current in practice and transferable across settings. An action-oriented approach helps to facilitate evaluation and review of your practice. Case studies are used throughout to enhance this process and to illustrate key points.

Research indicates that social workers vary considerably in the extent to which they make and test hypotheses in practice (Sheppard, et al., 2001). A shift towards understanding 'knowledge as process' as opposed to 'knowledge as product' is suggested as one way to integrate theory and practice. These changes to social work education and the recent shift to degree courses mean that there is a need for new, practical learning support material to help you achieve the qualification. This book is designed to help you gain knowledge about international perspectives on social work, to reflect on that knowledge and apply it in practice. The emphasis in this book is on enabling you to achieve the requirements of the curriculum and develop knowledge that assists you in meeting the Occupational Standards for social work.

Terminology

In your reading of material relevant to social work, you may have already begun to realise that in the study of social science and social work, there is rarely one straightforward definition of a concept, and gaining an understanding of international social work is not a straightforward matter. It might be helpful at this point to discuss some of the terminology we have decided to use in this book. The IFSW definition of social work above illustrates that the tasks and contexts in which social work occurs are varied and the workers engaging in those roles operate under different professional titles. We have chosen to use the term *social work* as an umbrella heading to encompass all of those activities and *social worker* to refer to the professionals carrying out that work. There is a more detailed discussion of some of the titles and roles known as *social worker* in Chapter 1.

There have been a variety of terms used to describe the developed and less developed countries (LDC) of the world. These have changed over time and in response to political shifts and movements (see for example Healy, 2001, p14). In this book, we use the terms 'Northern'/'Southern' countries to refer to the more industrialised countries located mainly in the Northern Hemisphere (but including Australia and New Zealand, geographically located in the south) and the developing economies mainly in the Southern Hemisphere. As Healy (2001) points out, these terms should be considered more political than geographical. The same can be applied to the use of the term 'The West' or 'Western' to describe developed or industrialised countries. However, when quoting from other sources, we have kept the variety of other terms used to describe the different classification of nations.

We use the term 'elders' in this book, as in many countries it recognises wisdom and denotes respect for older members of a society, in contrast to other more ageist terminology. Other acceptable terms such as 'older people' or 'seniors', where quoted by other commentators, have been retained. Further discussion of definitions relating to elders can be found in Chapter 6.

The Glossary at the end of this book provides some further definitions, as the variety and usage of words, as well as the numerous acronyms used in an international social work context, can be confusing.

That is why, in the first of the eight chapters of this book, we introduce you to some of the definitions of international social work and consider why an international perspective is increasingly important for social workers. We then go on to provide a discussion of values and ethics in the context of international issues and chart the more recent global and European developments making this a vital component of the social work landscape.

In Chapter 2 we discuss globalisation as a concept and how global movements – knowledge, people, capital – impact on all aspects of social work. We focus upon migration and issues that arise from people movement. You are asked to explore some of the factors that make people migrate, and invited to consider your own family history to explain how we are all international. We link the structural with the personal and emphasise that migration is not new and includes the sending of welfare cases 'away' (e.g. children and 'criminals' being sent to Australia). We go on to explore some common assumptions (other's and our own) about issues such as social security and the new EU migrants.

In Chapter 3 you are asked to consider how to utilise an international perspective using knowledge, skills and values outlined in Chapters 1 and 2. We go on to offer an international perspective on demography, to examine the various ways in which social services are organised and to explore different ideas about 'the family'. We then discuss developing skills in working cross-culturally, and give as an example working through interpreters. In the following four chapters in this book, international dimensions concerning specific service user groups are discussed, using activities, case studies, reflections and research to give examples and illustrate the many ideas being considered.

Chapter 4 explores different definitions of childhood and how childhood is socially constructed by different cultures and asks what factors constitute a good childhood. It goes on to discuss what children have a right to and what they need, before discussing international issues in assessing children and families. It asks when childhood ends and adulthood begins and explores the activities associated with childhood, youth and adulthood. International perspectives in issues such as adoption, child labour, child soldiers and the trauma of war will be considered. Finally, the notion of children's rights in different countries and the UN Convention on the Rights of the Child will be discussed.

Chapter 5 concerns mental health – different definitions of mental well-being are discussed along with some definitions of mental illness, including information from the World Health Organisation. Consideration is given in this chapter to social and biomedical models of mental disorder in different cultures and the impact service users have in shaping our understanding of mental ill health. Social and economic risk factors are explored, drawing from examples of people in different difficult situations. A discussion follows on the impact of stress, life changes and adverse attitudes such as racism for black and minority ethnic groups. Finally, some examples of 'mental health' policy in different countries are examined.

Differing definitions of 'old' are considered in Chapter 6, alongside the issue of ageing populations and emerging population trends in different countries. You are asked to explore views of elders from different social and cultural perspectives. Issues about incomes and work, pensions and other financial support for elders are discussed. We explore the nature of social work with elders, incorporating international issues and using case examples. Consideration is given to patterns of living in the UK – where do elders live and who do they live with? How does this compare with other countries and what are the trends and developments? These questions are considered alongside issues of migration and its impact on elders.

In Chapter 7, we ask who are people with disabilities and what are the difficulties in defining disability internationally? We discuss global issues such as poverty, war, employment and the structure of families to accommodate differences. The 'at risk' groups of people with disabilities in the UK are considered alongside issues such as class, being a member of a minority ethnic group, access to education, equality and the wider environment. Issues of exclusion and employment for people with disabilities are discussed in this context. In other countries, factors that are explored include poverty, development and disability. Social work, group work and work with communities of disabled people in the UK are discussed and we ask whether social work with people with disabilities is different in other countries, using examples to illustrate different approaches.

Chapter 8 introduces some new material about the history of social work as an international activity and links this to further material about international professional associations and employing organisations. The chapter also suggests a growing trend towards labour mobility and thus the internationalisation of the social professional workforce; and some summary points are made. In addition, the chapter also contains a short concluding section, which highlights some of the main points made in this book as a whole. There is an opportunity to chart your own learning in order to increase your knowledge, understanding and ability to apply this learning to practice. We also encourage you to reflect creatively on how your immediate learning needs can be met in developing an international perspective and how such a perspective can be enhanced through continuing professional development in your future career.

Chapter 1

Understanding international social work

Janet E Williams and Graeme Simpson

ACHIEVING A SOCIAL WORK DEGREE

This chapter will help you to become familiar with the following National Occupational Standards for Social Work.
Key Role 6: Demonstrate professional competence in social work practice.
Unit 18 Research, analyse, evaluate, and use current knowledge of best social work practice.
Unit 20 Manage complex ethical issues, dilemmas and conflicts.
Unit 21 Contribute to the promotion of best social work practice.

It will also introduce you to the following academic standards set out in the Quality Assurance Agency social work subject benchmark statement.
4. Defining principles.
4.3 (...)
- Social work is located within different social welfare contexts. (...) In an international context, distinctive national approaches to social welfare policy, provision and practice have greatly influenced the focus and content of social work degree programmes.
- There are competing views in society at large on the nature of social work and on its place and purpose. Social work practice and education inevitably reflect these differing perspectives on the role of social work in relation to social justice, social care and social order.
5. Subject knowledge, understanding and skills.
5.1.1 Social work services, service users and carers.
- the social processes (associated with, for example, poverty, migration, unemployment, poor health, disablement, lack of education and other sources of disadvantage) that lead to marginalisation, isolation and exclusion, and their impact on the demand for social work services.
5.1.2 The service delivery context.
- the location of contemporary social work within historical, comparative and global perspectives, including European and international contexts;
- the issues and trends in modern public and social policy and their relationship to contemporary practice and service delivery in social work.
5.1.3 Values and ethics.
- the complex relationships between justice, care and control in social welfare and the practical and ethical implications of these, including roles as statutory agents and in upholding the law in respect of discrimination.
5.1.4 Social work theory.
- the relevance of sociological perspectives to understanding societal and structural influences on human behaviour at individual, group and community levels.
5.1.5 The nature of social work practice.
- the place of theoretical perspectives and evidence from international research in assessment and decision-making processes in social work practice.

Introduction

In this chapter we explore definitions of international social work and address the question of why it is relevant to social workers. We will introduce you to themes used throughout the book such as 'the local is global is local', the significance of journeys and social work's value base. We look at social work in different environments and consider the values, aims and practices each one incorporates, asking whether or not social work is the same in all parts of the world. The chapter concludes with a list of resources, policies, and the addresses of international organisations to which you can refer as you 'internationalise' your everyday practice.

Exploring definitions of international social work

In this section we introduce you to ways of understanding and thinking critically about international social work. International social work is not a single concept or activity, nor is there total agreement about what it is or should be. From current definitions we can identify four aspects.

1. Social work is an international profession because there is an interchange of ideas and people across the world, supported by professional international organisations.

2. Social workers engage with people affected by international events, which means they undertake *internationally related domestic practice* (Healy, 2001, p7), reflected in the term used throughout this book, 'the local is global is local'.

3. The profession is required to challenge injustice by advocating for the oppressed and by influencing policy, not only locally but also internationally.

4. International practice is an identifiable element of social work because it takes place, in response to global events, through employment in international organisations such as the United Nations or the Red Cross and Red Crescent.

Healy (2001, p7) offers this definition:

> *International social work is defined as international professional practice and the capacity for international action by the social work profession and its members. International action has four dimensions: internationally related domestic practice and advocacy, professional exchange, international practice, and international policy development and advocacy.*

Gray and Fook say that it is a *social work that crosses national boundaries* (2004, p630) and which focuses on:

> *issues of international concern (for example, the problem of refugees, or ecological issues) and/or the way these are worked with at either international or domestic levels. It can refer to social work activities that take place at a global or international level (for example, work with international level organisations). It can also include activities involving international exchanges.*

An international profession

We begin by examining what we mean by social work as an 'international profession'. An international perspective not only informs you about what happens elsewhere, but it allows you to think about your own situation differently (Cochrane and Clarke, 1993). So, internationalising your social work practice can enable you to think of ways of doing things differently in practice in a local situation.

As with all professions social work has changed and developed through the exchange of ideas, and by comparing practice and policies across national boundaries, cultures and traditions. In this way new ideas are debated, promoted and disseminated widely and the profile of the profession is raised. This occurs through international conferences, writing, research and the exchange of social worker practitioners, educators, students, service users and carers, and was marked as early as 1928 with the first international social work conference in Paris (Lyons, 1999). Many organisations support this activity at all levels, regionally and globally, including the International Federation of Social Workers (IFSW) and the International Association of Schools of Social Work (IASSW).

An example of how ideas originating in one part of the world can impact in another is Family Group Conferencing, a system for supporting children. Its origins lie in the traditions of the Maori culture in New Zealand, but it has been tried and modified in several countries including England and the USA. Another example is the Patients' Councils in mental health hospitals which were started in the Netherlands by service users and were taken up by service users in the UK.

A benefit of comparing practice and policies is that it helps us to question our own taken for granted practice. Adoption is promoted in the UK to provide children with permanence, yet in Norway, where there is a high level of investment in preventative work to maintain children with their families, adoption is seen very differently. In 2005 there were a total of 890 adoptions, of which 79 per cent were of children born overseas; 15.5 per cent were step-parent adoptions and only 5.5 per cent, just 48, included foster parent adoptions and other types of adoption (Statistics Norway, 2007). This is an example where evidence for good practice has been interpreted in very different ways. Comparative social work, however, has to be more than borrowing ideas wholesale because social work practice is a culturally specific response to culturally defined social problems; it is essentially a *local* activity. This means that the way we think about, or even define a problem, may differ between countries, and so do the ways we conceptualise solutions.

When we engage in comparisons we need to understand the impact of power relations and imperialism, as discussed in Chapter 2. We see that economically powerful countries, which are often referred to as *Northern* countries, have considerable influence over less economically developed *Southern* countries; this influence is evident sometimes in social work. This has resulted in social work values and practice often being linked to the liberal democratic political values of the Northern countries which focus on *individual* freedom. In many cultures group cohesion, centred on the family, religious organisation, community or kin, may be of greater importance than the individual. We would expect social work in these countries to focus on or be mediated by the group, in contrast to traditional practice in the UK.

Some of the examples in this chapter are from countries where practice is less well resourced, and is more community orientated, to remind us that innovative practice occurs everywhere. We have already suggested that there is no single form of social work and this is also true within Europe, as illustrated by the range of terms given to social workers. Each title refers to a specific, local meaning, approach and set of responsibilities. The title *assistente sociale* is used in Italy and *social pedagogue* in parts of central and northern Europe. For convenience, sometimes all of the different titles are grouped under the broader heading of social professional (Lorenz, 1994).

The term pedagogue is used in many European countries. It usually describes practitioners who work with children and young people (though not exclusively with these groups) and in many instances they are called *social pedagogues*. For English speakers the terms are very difficult to translate and reflect a different cultural and historical approach to aspects of what we would term the social work task. Social pedagogy is drawn from the concept of education in its widest sense. One of the more recent attempts to define the term has been offered by Petrie, et al. (2006) who see it as a holistic response to providing care for children and young people. In many parts of Germany and some other Central and North European countries, social pedagogues also work with elders, again using a holistic approach. Petrie *et al.* emphasise the *whole person* approach and stress the vital importance of building positive and meaningful relationships with people. The essential elements of social pedagogy, wherever it is practised, incorporate the following:

- a pedagogy of relationships – the heart;
- listening – the ear;
- a pedagogy of reflection – the head;
- a practical pedagogy – the hands.

Social pedagogy represents a different way of doing social work which is located within the educational and social traditions of mainland Europe. Although it varies in form between countries, these four principles can be found wherever it is practised.

The local is global is local

In this book we argue that international social work is everyday practice for social workers because what happens abroad impacts on the local communities where we work, hence the phrase 'the local is global is local'. Everyone – social workers, service users and carers – is part of a global network and is touched directly or indirectly by what happens in other parts of the world. This is what we mean when we talk about *globalisation*. Globalisation has many different manifestations for social workers. You may be working in a team with social workers who were trained and have practised elsewhere and who were recruited to work in the UK because of a national shortage of social workers. You may have family members living elsewhere or you may be learning alongside people who were born or have previously lived elsewhere. Many of the service users and carers in your locality did not begin their lives there. All of these people have made journeys, an idea discussed further in this chapter. Your role as a social worker involves understanding the reasons for, and the impact of, their journeys.

A profession responding to international social problems

Another perspective on international social work is that we belong to a profession which concerns itself with international questions such as ecological disasters, civil war and economic deprivation. Such events trigger the mass movement of people and the international trade in people, which is now a more lucrative 'business' than illicit drug trafficking. The impact of these events becomes the responsibility of more than one nation state because they result in the movement of people (Healy, 2001). This approach raises some profound questions for social workers and how they respond to social problems. Though on a very different scale to the Indonesian tsunami of 2004, the floods in New Orleans in 2005, or those in China in 2008, the flooding during the summer of 2007 in England had a similar impact. It changed land use, and individuals, families and communities experienced death, disruption and destruction.

Now that we have discussed some aspects of international social work, consider your responses to these questions and return to them as you read through the book.

- Should the social work profession be advocating for oppressed groups as Healy (2001, p7) suggests?

- Do social workers have a responsibility to campaign to influence policies in countries other than their own, and if so how should they do this? (For example, they might wish to campaign against the widespread aborting of female foetuses in India or China).

- Should the profession advocate for the rights for women who are trafficked into sexual slavery, so that they obtain protection (rather then being sent back home as illegal migrants into the hands of the criminal gangs who run the business)?

- Do you think that changing or developing policies, also described as policy practice (Weiss, 2005), is part of social work practice?

International practice in international organisations

International organisations such as the Red Cross and Red Crescent, Oxfam and Christian Aid are present in circumstances of disaster to provide immediate and ongoing assistance, but they are also involved in development work. Social workers are employed to help displaced persons and to assist communities in addressing the social problems brought on by mass migration, civil war or the impact of HIV and AIDS. These are situations where individually focused work is not the norm and which may be challenging for social workers who come from individualistic traditions.

Commonalities and differences in social work globally

ACTIVITY 1.1

Think about the following questions:

- *Is the social work that you are familiar with locally the same as that carried out in different parts of the world?*

- *Is there something in common that all social workers would recognise in each other's practice wherever they found themselves?*

Comment

It might be useful to record your immediate responses to these questions and then return to them as you read through the book.

The members of the International Federation of Social Workers (IFSW) recognise that there are different roots to social work but beneath the differences there is a commonality of universal values.

> *Social work grew out of humanitarian and democratic ideals, and its values are based on respect for the equality, worth, and dignity of all people. Since its beginnings over a century ago, social work practice has focused on meeting human needs and developing human potential. Human rights and social justice serve as the motivation and justification for social work action. In solidarity with those who are disadvantaged, the profession strives to alleviate poverty and to liberate vulnerable and oppressed people in order to promote social inclusion.*
>
> *(IFSW, 2000)*

The following activity can help us to look at some of the differences and to identify what there may be in common to support the IFSW view that social work has a *universal application*.

ACTIVITY 1.2

What would your priorities be as the social worker in the two towns outlined below, and how might they differ between the two locations?

Nbandaka is a town in a wealthy country where there is full employment for men and women and a safety net of services for those unable to work. There are newcomers to the town who are attracted by the range of employment opportunities and some have arrived with qualifications from outside the region or abroad. There are some tensions between the newcomers and those who have been resident longer.

Queenstown is a town where the levels of poverty and child mortality are very high due to high unemployment and illiteracy rates. Queenstown is close to the borders of a country disturbed by civil war from which many refugees have fled. There is now a shortage of clean water as a result of the increase in population and new wells need to be sunk.

Comment

In both examples there may be common concerns related to the influx of new residents and the impact on the community, which might lead you to think about ways of improving community relations. There may be discrimination against the newcomers in employment protection, health and housing. International events have brought about the changes in both towns, and affect the social work task.

There are also some significant differences between Nbandaka and Queenstown related to wealth. As a social worker you would not be so concerned about a shortage of resources in Nbandaka but this would be one of your prime concerns for Queenstown. This in turn could mean that you make contact with regional or national governments and even international organisations. You would be alert to the low levels of education among Queenstown's residents. How confident or competent do local people feel about taking on the challenge of confronting politicians and approaching potential funding organisations? Should outsiders come in and take on the task, or are there means for developing the residents' skills, a process referred to as capacity building?

Let us look a little more closely at community- and group-orientated practices which were mentioned earlier in the chapter because some of the approaches would be useful, especially, but not exclusively, in Queenstown. Social development, or community development, is a form of social work which has the explicit aim of achieving social justice and addressing mass poverty through activities such as income generation, promoting social cohesion and capacity building (Cox and Pawar, 2006). Capacity building is closely related to empowerment because it operates on many levels. It includes enhancing self-esteem and confidence, learning and using new skills effectively, as well as focusing on structural problems in society. Capacity building can be focused on individuals, families, communities, local organisations, local government, civil society organisations, state institutions and even the private sector (Cox and Pawar, 2006, p83). In all contexts practitioners aim to build self-reliance, sustainability, participation, equity and human rights. The capacities vary according to context, so for example in Queenstown these would include literacy and basic education for individuals. At a group or community level it might mean ensuring that people have skills in setting up and running organisations for themselves, project management and researching sources of help, advice and funding. Social workers and service users would need to work within their organisations both *horizontally* and *vertically,* according to Gray and Fook (2004). Horizontal activity is about linking with informal and formal networks which deal with health, education, crime, religion as well as community organisations. Vertical activity on the other hand requires skills to engage with people in senior positions locally, regionally, nationally and sometimes internationally.

The examples in Activity 1.2 illustrate the difficulty of imposing a single model of social work practice on all communities. It might seem paradoxical when arguing in favour of the concept of international social work that social workers should focus on local conditions. However, when social workers apply theory to practice, they focus on people and their environment. This means that locality and culture (Lorenz, 1994, p45) and time and place (Lyons, 1999, p2), are important concepts for social work practice.

Who benefits from international social work and what do we need to know about?

We have given a number of reasons to support the idea that social work is an international activity and that we can improve our practice by learning from different social work traditions. We, and others in this book, argue that service users and carers benefit directly in everyday practice when social workers understand and apply international perspectives.

ACTIVITY 1.3

In the two examples that follow think about:

- which social work values are essential in these situations;

- how international perspectives might help you to understand the situation;

- what other knowledge and skills would be important.

Ali is a young man who has arrived in Europe from Iraq; he has fled torture and experienced the loss of his family. Portia, who is 60 years old, came from Jamaica and has lived in your country for the past 45 years. She was looked after in Jamaica by her grandmother when her parents left and she joined them when she was 15 years old. She has always wanted and expected to return 'home', to Jamaica. She is beginning to realise, reluctantly, that a return might not be possible because she no longer has any roots there.

Comment

For both Ali and Portia you may need to set aside your usual assumptions about daily life, unless you share the same background. You will need to learn about working sensitively in other people's cultures. This does not mean that you have to become an expert but you have to recognise that you might misunderstand situations because people construct events and meanings in ways that are unfamiliar to you, and vice versa. Language may be used differently or you may need to understand how best to work with an interpreter. You need to make sure that people can inform you about what is significant for them and that you can listen, without prejudice, to what they say.

For both Ali and Portia you will need to understand the political and economic reasons that produced their migrations, their assumptions when they arrived and their current expectations. In addition, for Ali and many people like him, you will need to learn about the effects of civil war and the realities of torture. The stereotypes about migrants in the press are mainly negative and you will need to challenge these and obtain facts, not fiction. It is not unusual for people who have survived and escaped the most dreadful circumstances in their own country to find the reception in the host country so confusing and discriminatory that they are (re-) traumatised. This understanding of oppression will give you the skills to look critically at your country's immigration policies. For the UK, the impact is outlined by Hayes and Humphries (2004) and specifically for young people by Kohli and Mather (2003). Other critiques, from a human rights perspective, can be found via national and international organisations concerned with refugees and asylum seekers, some of which are listed in the resources section at the end of this book.

Many of the theories used by social workers may be relevant for both Ali and Portia, including those relating to trauma, loss, resilience, and transitions, some of which relate to the idea of journeys through the life course. You cannot assume, however, that interventions in one culture, such as counselling, work in another and you should take care before you label a person with difficulties as mentally ill, on the basis of their expressing emotions in ways that make you feel uncomfortable. It is likely that Ali and Portia can be helped by people who have had similar experiences. There are specialist organisations for refugees and asylum seekers. For example, the Red Cross has expertise in finding and linking people who have become separated from family members.

From the questions and suggestions about social work with Ali and Portia, we have shown you how international perspectives can improve practice, and suggested some of the skills and theories that may help you to understand their situation and what might help them. There are some similarities in approach even though the two people may seem to be in very different circumstances.

There are also personal and professional benefits from adopting an international approach. If professionally you are open-minded and curious about why social workers practise differently elsewhere, then you could take the opportunity to study or practise in other European countries through the support available through the European Union (see the resources at the end of the book). If this is impossible you could offer to volunteer at a local organisation that works with immigrants so that you can learn how to become sensitive to their needs and develop skills for working with people from different cultures. Pringle (1998, p4) writes that *understanding the welfare systems of states entails gaining knowledge of their wider cultures, histories and their economic[s] ... one is ... engaged in emotional and intellectual voyages of discovery* and that it's fun!

Journeys in a global context

Pringle's comments lead us to one of the key conceptual themes of the book: journeys and the social work response to the people who have made them. Journeys can be geographical, as people move from place to place, as well as through the life course. Journeys are often made in response to economic conditions but these may be affected, for example, by the change in responsibilities between childhood and adulthood, or by becoming older. These transitions between life stages are usually manifested in culturally specific ways.

A geographical move may seem the only option to overcome economic, political or environmental problems, the causes of which may be linked to globalisation. The common characteristic of journeys, which involve leaving home, culture and family, is that they contain losses linked to identity and status, as well as gains. Migrants have to adapt to a new culture, and their presence in turn makes the host culture more diverse. Some journeys represent free choice; some are made as the least worst option; while others, often affecting women and children, are forced journeys through kidnapping, trafficking and deception.

When the movement from the homeland is extensive, involving mass migration, it is referred to as 'diaspora'. The term means 'scattering' and it usually takes place because of oppression, slavery or colonisation. The phenomenon of diaspora is a very ancient one and was first used to describe the expulsion of the Jews from Egypt in 587 BC and again, from other countries through the millennia and into the twentieth century. A recent diaspora is that of the Palestinian people, while those who have sought asylum recently in the UK include Chileans, Iraqis and Zimbabweans.

Some journeys are cross-national, such as to Nbandaka and Queenstown, and for Ali and Portia, while others are across regions within countries. There have been many mass movements of people within the UK for reasons of employment. When the coalfields opened and expanded in the nineteenth and early twentieth centuries, for home and global consumption, many people moved to the coalfields in Nottinghamshire and Derbyshire, and to South Wales. Since 1981 'get on your bike and look for work', misquoted from comments made by Conservative government minister Norman Tebbit, has been the prescription for people living in areas of high unemployment, such as the North of England, to move to more prosperous regions, predominantly London and the South-East.

There have been mass movements of people in the UK for more sinister reasons. The Scottish Highland clearances, in the late eighteenth and early nineteenth centuries, were the forced displacement of tens of thousands of people to make way for large-scale sheep farming. Houses and villages were destroyed to ensure that people moved away; many went to the coast and the Lowlands of Scotland, later to emigrate. More recently children of poor working-class parents in the UK were deported to Australia, Canada, New Zealand and to Zimbabwe, then known as Rhodesia (Parker, 2007). They were sent to populate the Commonwealth with white children and to save the UK the expense of looking after them, though many were not orphans. More than 130,000 children were 'exported' over a period of 100 years, until 1967, to work as farm labourers. People are still emigrating from the UK. For example, some have gone to Spain for retirement in the sun, where they are forming large communities that are becoming English-speaking enclaves among the Spanish population.

Social work values and ethics in an international context

In this section we want to return to the idea of international social work and social work values. There is general agreement about the significance of values in social work and this was expressed by a working party of two international social work organisations, IFSW and IASSW, which collectively wrote:

> *Ethical awareness is a fundamental part of the professional practice of social workers. Their ability and commitment to act ethically is an essential aspect of the quality of the service offered to those who use social work services.*

> (IFSW, 2004)

In moral philosophy values are about what is considered *good* or *bad* for people and thus they inform what social workers think they *ought* to do. Ethics, a related aspect of moral philosophy, is also concerned with values, what is right or wrong, and is often associated with formally constructed codes of conduct. The definition of social work from the IFSW and the IASSW shows how the aims of social work are based on values. They identify two fundamental principles – human rights and social justice – which can often raise dilemmas for social workers, wherever they are working.

Definition of social work (IASSW and IFSW, 2004)

> *The social work profession promotes social change, problem solving in human relationships and the empowerment and liberation of people to enhance well-being. Utilising theories of human behaviour and social systems, social work*

intervenes at the points where people interact with their environments.
Principles of human rights and social justice are fundamental to social work.

The activities at the heart of social work, such as promoting social change and problem-solving for individuals, communities and societies, have the potential to be both empowering and oppressive. This means that ... *neutrality is not possible, since any intervention necessarily represents some values* (Clarke, 2000, p3).

IFSW and IASSW give some reasons for the potential ethical pitfalls in social work practice.

- *The [...] loyalty of social workers is often in the middle of conflicting interests.*

- *[...] Social workers function as both helpers and controllers.*

- *[There are] conflicts between the duty of social workers to protect the interests of the people with whom they work and societal demands for efficiency and utility.*

- *[...] Resources in society are limited.*
(IFSW, 2004)

The two fundamental ethical principles, *human rights and dignity* and *social justice* are described in detail in Section 4 of the IFSW/IASSW statement and are outlined briefly below. We would argue that these values are the foundation of social work globally, although as Hugman (2007, pp20–29) points out they can be manifested in different ways depending on culture.

Here are the IFSW/IASSW definitions of these two ethical principles.

Human Rights and Human Dignity

Social work is based on respect for the inherent worth and dignity of all people, and the rights that follow from this. Social workers should uphold and defend each person's physical, psychological, emotional and spiritual integrity and well-being.

Social Justice

Social workers have a responsibility to promote social justice, in relation to society generally, and in relation to the people with whom they work.

(IFSW, 2004)

ACTIVITY **1.4**

Read the IFSW/IASSW Ethics in Social Work, Statement of Principles, which you can access at www.ifsw.org/en/p38000324.html. Are the principles it espouses familiar to you? Think about the following questions in relation to your local experience.

- *Do you or your organisation aim to bring about social change?*

- *Is your work based on helping people to solve problems in relationships?*

- *How much are you aware of working to defend people's human rights? Is this a concept that you are familiar with in social work?*

- *Do you think that social work in your country plays a part in actively challenging societal injustices, as well as those experienced by individuals and families?*

Comment

We will explore these ideas further by examining two examples of social work, one from Germany and the other from South Africa, and we will compare and contrast them with practice in the UK, and focus upon social development work and social pedagogy, which we have introduced earlier.

When we look at different countries it is often the case that people begin by identifying what is different and this is often determined by the context. We then identify what social workers may hold in common. As you read the following section, think through what you might have in common with social workers in these countries.

South Africa is a country undergoing transition, like many other Southern countries, and this is the case to a lesser extent (and in a different economic context) in Germany since reunification. South Africa is a country forging a new identity, along with its neighbours, by taking the best from its long history while questioning aspects of its European, colonial legacy such as apartheid. Unlike Germany and the UK it is not yet a modern, economically developed industrial country that can support an expensive, elaborate welfare state. For this reason the state cannot afford to be the main employer of social workers, nor does it yet provide a well-developed infrastructure of legislation, policy and education for all social work and social care workers. The voluntary sector is the main employer but the private sector is the fastest growing area where remedial psychologically-orientated work takes place with individuals, similar to the model of social work in the USA.

Some practitioners in South Africa are engaged in social development and social action models of community-orientated practice, described earlier (Mupedziswa, 2001; Norward, 2007). This approach aims to address social injustice and to bring about structural change in the social environment. This generally means working with identified groups such as the very poorest, those subject to violence, migrant labour and people with HIV/AIDS. Some of this activity is targeted at women because it is recognised that they are key actors in the development process, and in protecting and educating children. Although there is no well-resourced welfare structure the national policy context is particularly helpful for social work, because the constitution explicitly upholds human rights for everyone without exception.

In Germany, as in the UK, there is a well-developed system of welfare provision, but unlike the UK, it is largely located within the voluntary sector, which includes Catholic and Protestant churches and the trades unions as major providers of services. We have already seen how social pedagogy is a concept which would be very familiar to German social workers, but would be virtually unknown in the UK or in South Africa. The variety and types of organisations that social workers are employed in would also be quite different, with around 80 per cent of *qualified* social workers in Germany working for the voluntary sector, unlike the UK where local authority employment still dominates, and different again from South Africa. They also work in a different political and legislative framework. In Germany and the UK social workers operate in more formalised, institutional settings in which there are well-developed systems of accountability. In South Africa, because there is less infrastructure and funding, initiatives may come from community members with only limited support from social work and the state. An example would be where women in a community organise the support of orphaned children with HIV/AIDS. While there may be some funding to support this venture from social work organisations, the women running it would not be accountable to the state through social work regulations, police checks and monitoring such as exist for child care in Germany or the UK.

Once we can move away from these differences, the extent of what is shared quickly becomes clear. In Germany and the United Kingdom social workers generally work with the same groups of people who face difficulties – as we feature in the chapters of this book. This would be the case to some extent in South Africa but, as described above, there would also be more emphasis on communities.

Many of the methods used in Germany and South Africa are used elsewhere – indeed, German social workers would be familiar with many of the well-known British or American social work texts – either through translated versions or in the original, and these are used also by the majority of social workers in South Africa. Finally, what would emerge is a common set of motivations and values. There is a strong and shared desire to 'help people' or to 'make a difference'. They may all share similar political views about social justice and a need for action at a political level to address inequality, though this would not be the foremost activity for everyone. They would also share values about confidentiality, self-determination and the belief that some people need protection and support.

C H A P T E R   S U M M A R Y

In this chapter we have explained some of the key definitions that help us understand the concept of international social work, and why it is relevant to social workers everywhere.

- We explored the definitions of international social work and identified four of its key aspects. We offered two definitions, which both highlighted social work's concern with development and social justice; themes which run through the chapter, and the book as a whole.

- We developed some of the arguments for social work to be an international profession and explored how developing an international perspective has been a long-standing objective of many social workers. We also identified a number of international organisations which will be referred to throughout the book.

- We highlighted some of the difficulties, for example, different terminology (such as social pedagogues) and also different understandings of what is good practice (for example Norway and adoption).

- We introduced the concept of 'the global is local' and that social work is a profession which deals with a range of international problems. We also introduced the idea of journeys, both through the life course and also through migration, and how this impacts upon people. This theme is developed throughout the book.

- We then explored differences and commonalities in social work. We suggested that differences are often to do with local factors but that social workers in different parts of the world have much in common, especially when we talk about their value base.

Cox, D and Pawar, M (2006) *International social work: Issues, strategies and programs*. London: Sage Publications.

This is a more detailed account of international social work.

Hayes, D and Humphries, B (2004) *Social work, immigration and asylum*. London: Jessica Kingsley Publishers.

This book considers ethical and practical challenges facing social workers in practice with refugees, asylum seekers and other people who are subject to immigration control, and includes some perspectives on practice in other countries.

Humphreys, M (1996) *Empty cradles*. London: Corgi Adult.

This book is the story of child migrants to Australia as uncovered by Margaret Humphreys who was a social worker in Nottingham at the time. She established the Child Migrants Trust (see resources section at the end of this book).

Lavalette, M and Ferguson, I (eds) (2007) *International social work and the radical tradition*. Birmingham: Venture Press.

This book offers accounts of radical social work practice worldwide in developing and also developed countries.

Chapter 2
Global is local is global

Graeme Simpson and Sue Lawrence

A C H I E V I N G   A   S O C I A L   W O R K   D E G R E E

This chapter will help you to meet the following National Occupational Standards for Social Work.
Key Role 6: Demonstrate professional competence in social work practice.
Unit 18 Research, analyse, evaluate, and use current knowledge of best social work practice.
Unit 20 Manage complex ethical issues, dilemmas and conflicts.
Unit 21 Contribute to the promotion of best social work practice.

It will also introduce you to the following academic standards set out in the Quality Assurance Agency social work subject benchmark statement.
4. Defining principles.
4.3 (...)
- Social work is located within different social welfare contexts. (...) In an international context, distinctive national approaches to social welfare policy, provision and practice have greatly influenced the focus and content of social work degree programmes.
5. Subject knowledge, understanding and skills.
5.1.1 Social work services, service users and carers.
- the nature and validity of different definitions of, and explanations for, the characteristics and circumstances of service users and the services required by them, drawing on knowledge from research, practice experience, and from service users and carers.
5.1.2 The service delivery context.
- the location of contemporary social work within historical, comparative and global perspectives, including European and international contexts;
- the complex relationships between public, social and political philosophies, policies and priorities and the organisation and practice of social work, including the contested nature of these;
- the issues and trends in modern public and social policy and their relationship to contemporary practice and service delivery in social work.
5.1.4 Social work theory.
- research-based concepts and critical explanations from social work theory and other disciplines that contribute to the knowledge base of social work, including their distinctive epistemological status and application to practice;
- the relevance of sociological perspectives to understanding societal and structural influences on human behaviour at individual, group and community levels;
- social science theories explaining group and organisational behaviour, adaptation and change.

Introduction

We begin this chapter by examining the concept of globalisation, and aim to show that people's lives in the UK are affected by what happens elsewhere. This is what is meant by the idea that the *global is local*. We will explore globalisation on three levels, which are equally important and interrelated.

1. *Capital* – that is, financial markets and the way in which companies can invest in any country where they can get a high return. Thus, capital can be moved rapidly all over the world.

2. *Labour* – that is, people. Globalisation is not confined to the movement of money, but it also includes the movement of people between countries.

3. *Knowledge* – that is, information, ideas and skills and the ways in which these are now increasingly global and not confined to a particular country or continent.

As the chapter develops, each of these themes will be explored by using a combination of case studies, research summaries and exercises, which should enable you to make links between these different areas.

Globalisation and the movement of capital

It may seem a strange place to begin a study of global social work, but the movement of capital has a huge impact upon all of our daily lives. The events of September and October 2008 clearly demonstrate this. What began as being called 'the credit crunch' had, by October 2008, been referred to by the Japanese Prime Minister, Taro Aso, as a 'financial storm that comes along once every 100 years' (Elliot and McCurry, 2008).

The causes of the economic crisis were many and beyond the scope of this chapter, but we want to begin by identifying some of the implications of financial downturn for social work, both globally and locally.

Firstly, a lot less money is usually spent on 'welfare' or social services as a result. In an interview with *The Guardian*, Tony Travers of the London School of Economics speculated that there would be pressures upon public spending for ten years, because of the economic downturn. Evidence from previous recessions shows reductions in public spending (*The Guardian*, 2008). The initial response of Government in the UK was to argue for greater borrowing to ensure service provision. Ultimately though, money borrowed has to be paid back, and it is usually through a combination of tax rises and reduced expenditure. Social work has had to deal with this before, but it is arguable that demands for services, especially in relation to social care for elders and disabled people, is increasing due to ageing populations (see Chapter 6). A further demonstration of how interrelated the banking crisis and social services are was the amount of UK local authority money held in failed Icelandic banks. A series of BBC reports revealed that UK charities, local authorities and service providers had over £1 billion in Icelandic banks (BBC News, 2008a). Kent County Council had £50 million and Nottingham City Council £42 million (BBC News, 2008b). The likelihood is that this loss (if not fully recovered) would lead to job cuts and inevitable reductions in services in some councils (BBC News, 2008c).

Secondly, it is often the case that so-called 'social problems' increase during times of recession, which bring higher levels of unemployment, greater levels of relative poverty, and frequently result in higher levels of crime. In short, recessions accentuate pre-existing inequality and differentials between the rich and poor (Glyn, 2006). While crime statistics are difficult to interpret, Merton's (1957) theoretical approach, developed in the 1930s, suggests that it will increase; as do Marxist conflict theories of crime (Muncie, 1999). There is also evidence that in times of recession and deepening poverty, there is likely to be an increase in mental ill health (Pilgrim and Rogers, 1999). Durkheim's famous study (2002) also showed the extent to which suicide is linked to times of rapid social change.

Thirdly, the people who are usually hit the hardest by recessions are those who are poor. In developed economies, poor people experience job losses without the large pay-offs associated with banking executives. In October 2008, it was estimated that unemployment in the UK could reach 2 million by early 2009. In the underdeveloped Southern Hemisphere, the crisis impacted upon the long-term plans to reduce poverty overall. The signs were that pledges made on overseas aid and development would be threatened as increasingly governments turned their attention to their own economic difficulties (Elliot, 2008). Also, the economic situation in the developed Northern Hemisphere would impact upon the level of remittances to the south. Remittances refer to the money sent back to families in their country of origin by overseas workers. While these remittances were high ($251 billion in 2007) there was evidence that remittances from the USA to Mexico and Central America were slowing down (Ratha, et al., 2008).

One of the more common consequences of the movement of capital however is job losses, and this has been a feature of the economic climate since the mid 1990s. Read the following case study, which provides an example of how low-paid workers in Scotland have lost their jobs, and how many more of them are under threat of redundancy because of decisions made by the companies they work for.

CASE STUDY

In September 2006, a major UK financial group announced a total of 4,500 job losses in its UK operations. Of these 450 were to be in its Scottish call centres. The centre in Perth was the most affected, a location where the insurance industry has traditionally had a substantial base, and which is particularly dependent upon the 'call centre economy'. Scotland is itself a relatively small country, where the call centre has become a significant form of employment, due mainly to Scotland's low wage and high skills economy. In 2005 over 60,000 people were employed in call centres and Scotland had not been subject to high levels of the outsourcing of jobs to India. Nationally the job losses were to be offset by the relocation of workers within the UK. The company aimed to save £50 million annually from the operation. It had recently announced half-year profits of £1.7 billion.

(Sources: Bowker, 2005; *The Scotsman* Business, 2006; Ross and Brown, 2006)

Within this case study there are several points about the impact of globalisation, which are directly related to the movement of capital. First, the rationale for the so-called outsourcing is to maximise the company's profits by using cheaper labour. The investment in the

Indian subcontinent is primarily to ensure greater profitability, and not to develop the economy of that region. Second, the actual 'savings', although significant in themselves, are small when compared to the overall profits. Third, there will not only be a relocation of the call centres, which will result in job losses in Scotland and other parts of the UK, but also the need for some workers to relocate within the UK. On the other hand, more jobs are created for workers in India as a result and with this comes better paid work for many people there. Finally, there will be considerable effects upon people's lives in Scotland, the UK and also India as a result of decisions taken based upon the movement of 'capital' and the desire to maximise profit. Jobs will be moved on the decision of managers whose primary responsibility is towards generating profit and not to the workforce. So, in this sense, what is often regarded as a global question has a direct impact upon the 'local'.

For social workers there are at least two important points to consider in relation to this aspect of globalisation. First, the consequences of losing a job and the resulting unemployment can act as a trigger for difficulties in people's lives that could result in social work involvement. Unemployment means a reduced income and this impacts negatively on people's lives. While being poor is not in itself a basis for social work involvement in the UK, many of the people who social workers deal with are poor. A full range of factors, including poor health, greater likelihood of accidents in the home, poor diet and increased stress levels are associated with poverty. There is increasing evidence that mental ill health can be triggered by losing a job and the resulting lowering of self-esteem that this brings about. Second, the movement of labour within the UK (and for that matter in India, since workers move to cities to find better paid work) can result in higher levels of isolation since invariably this means moving away from family and friends.

ACTIVITY 2.1

Think about your own family at this point and ask the question whether or not family members have always lived in the same place? Have family members always lived in the same country (remember, for the purpose of this activity, there are four countries which make up the UK: England, Wales, Scotland and Northern Ireland)? If the answer is 'yes', have your family members always lived in the same locality? Then consider why people moved and how many of these moves were based around getting work. If people stayed in the same place, why was that?

Comment

It is likely that most people reading this chapter will have identified some relocation within their family. There could well be several reasons identified as to why people moved or stayed put, but we would imagine that for most people one of the reasons was related to finding work or improving work prospects. Even within a single country, people may have moved from the area of their birth to a completely different area to find work which drew on their existing skills. For example, within the UK, the town of Corby in Northamptonshire has a very large population of Scottish origin, since the steelworks recruited workers from the steel towns of Scotland. Of course, the steelworks in Corby has now closed, as steel production has been relocated to other countries where labour is cheaper. Another example is the large Irish population in the UK, many of whose families originally came over in the migration of the 1840s as a result of the 'famine'. We can also see that many of the great movements of people, particularly within the UK, were connected to times of economic hardship and recession, which is a further factor to consider as part of the global 'credit crunch' in 2008, with which we began the chapter. For many people in the UK their country of origin will be overseas, and it is to this subject that we now turn.

RESEARCH SUMMARY

The research carried out by human geographers at the University of Sheffield has focused upon 'spatial inequality' and has also built upon the known links between poverty and black and minority ethnic (BME) groups. Dorling and Thomas's book, People and Places: A 2001 census atlas of the UK *(2004) provides an account of the census data through 'cartograms', that is maps which visualise areas where poverty is concentrated, and which show the geographic distribution of different ethnic groups within the UK. One of the features they investigate is the changing relationship between the generations, demonstrating how the age groups are moving away from each other geographically. Their research also shows how traditional jobs are disappearing as a result of industry moving out of the UK into other countries, notably China. We suggest this confirms the links between the movement of capital and people's lives. However, the work undertaken by human geographers also illustrates another example of global forces at work: migration.*

Based upon work carried out at the University of Sheffield and the Institute for Public Policy Research, the BBC has developed a website which shows where people live who were 'born abroad' and are now resident in the UK. According to 2001 census figures, 7.5 per cent of UK residents were born abroad. The 'born abroad' category measures where people were born and not their 'ethnicity', since a high proportion of the UK's BME group population was born in the UK. Given the recent increased movement of labour within the European Union, it is possible that the actual current figure of 'born abroad' residents is higher. The data shows very clearly that a high proportion of migrants are in poorly paid jobs, which indicates the growing demand for cheap labour. The website contains some very useful information about the impact of global forces at a local level and the address can be found in the resources section at the end of this book.

Globalisation and the movement of people: Migration

Migration is perhaps one of the main areas where we can connect global and local questions. It is also one area in which social work can be said to be truly 'international'. Social workers in the UK will encounter people who are recent migrants to the UK, and so it is important that they develop the knowledge base to understand this aspect of how the global impacts upon the local, and how they need to utilise aspects of this in developing their own practice. While we have focused upon migration to the UK, it is important to note that 5.5 million British people live permanently overseas (Sriskandarajah and Drew,

2006). Figures from the Office of National Statistics reported that in 2006 over 200,000 people born in the UK left for other countries. Many were leaving the UK to seek a warmer climate and a 'better lifestyle', while some were returning to their country of birth. This data helps us understand that there are other 'push' and 'pull' factors here and that the UK is also a country that still has a high level of emigration, as well as the more regularly reported immigration (Curtis, 2007).

Migration is also a question that has been a focus of interest for political parties. The accession of Romania and Bulgaria to the EU on 1 January 2007 has resulted in the UK imposing quotas for migrants from these countries, and strict guidelines for entry, as migration as an issue is seized upon by populist politicians. It is therefore necessary for social workers to understand the background to migration and to have a sense of the factors which impact upon it.

Studies of migration typically identify what are called 'push–pull' factors, which explain why people move. Importantly, however, we would stress that there is both the push and the pull; it is not just about those forces which either encourage or drive people to leave their country of origin – the 'push' factors – but also there are 'pull' factors associated with the country of destination. We will discuss the expansion of the EU later, but first we will explore other potential push-pull factors that affect recent migrants to the UK. It is fair to say that migration covers all aspects of the movement of people from one country to another. Often this is done through the acquisition of work permits in order to take up a job the migrant has already secured; sometimes the migrant wishes to join existing family members who live in that country; sometimes the reason for moving is to seek asylum, that is to claim a residence in a country because the country of origin is no longer safe. Asylum seekers are frequently the cause of much public debate. On a global scale only a minority of the world's asylum seekers arrive in Europe. The United Nations estimate that globally there are over 20 million refugees and internally displaced people (someone who has fled their home usually as a consequence of war) worldwide. Usually people flee to bordering countries, therefore most 'migration' in this sense is 'south to south'. A recent example is that more than 300,000 asylum seekers are estimated to be in the Middle East as a result of the Iraq conflict, many of whom moved to Jordan. The number of asylum seekers to the UK between January and March 2008 was 7,705 in total and 6,595 excluding dependants, the top five nationalities being Afghan, Iraqi, Zimbabwean, Iranian and Eritrean. A total of 3,025 asylum applicants were removed from the UK in the same quarter (Home Office, 2008).

If we look at the countries of origin of many asylum applicants, we can see that a significant push factor is war. Frequently this is civil war, associated with internal political upheaval. In other countries we can see that people often flee to escape repressive regimes. Across the world we have seen different forms of 'ethnic cleansing' which has led to people seeking asylum and refugee status. These are both substantial 'push' factors in relation to migration.

A clear migration 'pull' factor takes us back to the first section in this chapter, that is, the demand for cheap labour. There is a range of anecdotal evidence about the extent of unregulated, undocumented or 'illegal' labour in many EU countries. We want to stress that this is a 'pull' factor – the demand for cheap labour already exists; it is not created by the arrival of people seeking work. We would also add that another pull factor for the UK is the worldwide dominance of English as a language. Many people choose the UK in preference to other European countries because they can speak the language. The existence of established groups of people of different national origins in the UK also provides a further pull factor: many people can find an existing 'community' from their country of origin. The presence of well-established BME communities in many countries, including the countries of the UK, can be traced from the colonial relationships that existed in the past. The demand for cheap labour, as well as highly skilled professionals to address skills shortages, was often dependent upon colonial (and often very unequal) relationships, where a common language and special migration arrangements were in place.

When considering pull factors, and the need for cheap labour, we come to another aspect of migration: people trafficking. The term 'people trafficking' means the illegal movement of people from one country to another for profit. There are many instances of this in recent times, and one of the main areas relates to the illegal trafficking of women, who are brought from abroad, often with the promise of legal work and a better future, and are then forced into sex work or prostitution. In October 2006, a centre in Sheffield was opened to work with people (mainly women) who had been the victims of people trafficking. The centre combines the work of academics and experts in different areas, who all work together to support people who have been the victims of trafficking. In opening the centre, Mike O'Brien, the Solicitor-General, said:

> *Some victims do not even realise they are being trafficked until they arrive and then find the job they were promised as a waitress turns out to be enforced servitude as a prostitute, including being beaten and raped. Today in London I am told that trafficked women can be bought and sold for as little as £3,000 each. They often live in terror, believing that if they try to escape their pimps will kill them.*
>
> (BBC News, 2006a)

The centre had been opened as a result of an extensive police operation, which 'rescued' 84 women and 12 children from Africa, Malaysia, Thailand and Eastern Europe. Thus, in this area, social workers and allied professionals will have a key role. Within the UK, not many professionals with the title 'social worker' routinely see asylum seekers although many social workers deal with asylum seekers. As we will see in other chapters of this book, this global question is increasingly becoming part of the background to much UK-based social work. Within other countries asylum seekers are routinely in contact with social workers. Work with people who have experienced trauma and loss is very much part of 'local' practice, yet as this section demonstrates it originates from global factors.

People trafficking can have very severe consequences. The women and children at the Sheffield centre had, according to one interviewee, been subjected to rape and abuse up to 30 times each day (BBC News, 2006a). Another form of illegal movement of people is 'people smuggling'. People often pay huge sums of money to attain a better life in the West, but on arrival they experience poor working conditions, exploitation, and for some even more severe consequences.

In February 2004, 23 Chinese cockle pickers lost their lives in Morecambe Bay. Workers from China, who had been recruited as illegal labour and controlled by gang-masters, were transported from Liverpool to the north Lancashire town to pick cockles in the notorious waters of Morecambe Bay. As the tide came in they became completely cut off, and while a few escaped, the majority drowned. At the trial of the gang-masters, who were convicted and imprisoned, it emerged that many of the Chinese pickers had telephoned their loved ones in China as they faced death. They were not all aware of how they could contact emergency services, although one of them did. One gang-master was sentenced to 14 years' imprisonment and his two co-accused were sentenced to four and two years. During the trial it was suggested that the Immigration Service knew about the illegal gang-masters but did nothing about it.

(Sources: Casciani, 2005; BBC News, 2006b)

The story of the Morecambe Bay cockle pickers demonstrates how people trafficking is driven by economic exploitation. The Chinese cockle pickers were low-paid workers, who had paid large amounts of money to be trafficked illegally into the UK. Once here, they endured highly dangerous working conditions and were paid very low wages. The local tragedy in Morecambe Bay was truly global as it impacted upon their partners and children on the other side of the world.

What we can see in the study of globalisation in relation to the movement of capital and people is that it is driven by a desire to make a profit. This may take the relatively benign form of relocating jobs within a country, resulting in the movement of people within national borders. It may mean the loss of jobs in one country where workers are seen as 'too expensive'. At its extreme it results in the illegal trafficking of people, either for sexual exploitation or into highly exploitative work. Social work at both a local and global level frequently deals with people who have experienced trauma and upheavals in their lives as a consequence of these aspects of globalisation and so this is of central importance for the twenty-first-century practitioner, who can no longer ignore the global picture.

Globalisation and knowledge

The third aspect of globalisation we want to examine is the *globalisation of knowledge*. Bell (1980) was one of the early writers to explore how the development of information technology would impact upon people's lives and others have developed these ideas, notably Castells (2001). First, one of the more obvious features of the globalisation of knowledge is the speed and ease with which people can get news. The use of mobile phone technology means that almost anyone can take pictures of a 'news event'. Ordinary people can become eyewitnesses and provide images for others. In this way it could be suggested that such developments have led to a greater degree of participation in newsgathering.

Second, not only can we gather and disseminate news quickly, there is also a much greater quantity of information that is available to us. We can be aware of events in countries the other side of the world within minutes and as such there is a sense in which it could be said that we experience 'information overload'. Many of the UK's Asian families are among those most likely to have satellite television (Bennett, et al., 2006) since through this they can not only watch entertainment in their own languages, but also discover how news is reported elsewhere.

Third, we suggest that the ease of communication through new technology has changed people's lives. Ease of communication has enabled the transfer of jobs, as outlined in the section about movement of capital. Without technological advances, call centres would not be able to relocate to different continents. In other ways the ease of communications allows families to keep in touch with members who have moved away to find work. In the case of the Chinese cockle pickers, they were able to use their mobile phones to speak their final words to loved ones in China. So, in a tangible way, communication technology has changed the nature of migration and allowed for contact to be more readily maintained. So social workers involved with people who have come from other countries can readily experience how 'local' takes on a 'global' meaning. The 'local' can also include places far away, especially with the rise of web-cam technology. We can see another aspect of this in the development of 'virtual' communities.

The virtual community is one that is not bounded by place, but rather shaped by common interest (Calhoun, 1998). The use of the internet not only allows families to maintain contact, but also allows for new communities with shared interests to be developed. We can join chat rooms or mailing lists that are hosted anywhere in the world in pursuit of an interest that can be shared globally. Such communities can also be the site of global marketing. For example, many football clubs market their 'brand' globally. Just as an English teenager can follow the fortunes of Barcelona, so a Korean can follow Manchester United. On the other hand, aspects of global communication can also have negative expressions, for example internet-based crime (identity fraud) and also the availability of exploitative images of children and women.

Finally, we want to suggest that while this aspect of globalisation has distinct benefits, especially in relation to migrant families, there is also the question of access. The development of global communication can be a force for inclusion, yet at the same time it can also act as a powerful force for marginalisation. So, if you do not have access to the technology, you cannot participate in it and therefore, for many people at the 'local' level, the 'global' remains distant. Yet events in other parts of the world and the movement of global capital and labour still shape their lives and life chances.

Drawing the threads together: Globalising culture

We have introduced three aspects of globalisation, which are central to understanding the connections between the local and global. In this section we want to suggest that they all converge in what has been called globalising culture. We will start with a brief summary of the work undertaken by the American sociologist, George Ritzer (1993) in his study of the global expansion of certain forms of American 'culture' and practices, which he termed *the McDonaldisation of society.*

RESEARCH SUMMARY

Ritzer argues that business has taken over the world of leisure and turned this into a form of culture that can be marketed. To do this on a global scale, certain features dominate: efficiency, calculability and predictability. Efficiency refers to the easiest way to achieve the aim of having a burger and Ritzer claims that in the fast food restaurant you 'choose' from a limited menu and diversions from this are not well received. Calculability is the emphasis upon quantity rather than quality and this culminates in the predictability of the product, the effort to enable people to know what to expect at all times and in all places ... a world that offers no surprises (1993, p99). This helps create the phenomenon of a globalised culture. Multinational enterprises dominate the landscape of all of the world's major cities. A key feature is the control of the product and the workforce, a simplification, or rationalisation, of production and the sanitisation of difference to ensure 'no surprises'. Ritzer argues that these are the defining features of the late twentieth century, which he equates to an iron cage moving irresistibly forwards, which should be resisted.

We have seen how globalisation can dominate all areas of people's lives including their leisure time and this is driven by the search for new markets and outlets to sell products. Of course, not all of the globalising of culture is negative. The spread of art and especially music throughout the world is one way in which we can see how global trends can impact upon local taste, without destroying diversity. The accessibility of 'world music' is an example of this, but often this is accompanied by the exploitation of indigenous musicians, who do not always receive their full reward. The 'global kitchen' is yet another example. While there are many different types of restaurant in the UK, lots of these present 'anglicised' food, rather than authentic cooking. The Chinese restaurant, which promotes the 'all you can eat buffet' for its English customers, usually offers a more authentic menu for the Chinese community.

ACTIVITY **2.2**

Think about Ritzer's arguments. Walk around your local town or city and try to work out which companies are 'global' and which are genuinely 'local'. Think about how 'culture' is packaged and marketed. Do you think this celebrates diversity or limits it?

Globalisation: New or old?

Much of the thinking around globalisation sees it as a new phenomenon. Certainly, the technological developments associated with it would imply that this is the case. Yet, we would suggest that while recent developments have increased the pace and impact of the global upon the local, there is nothing new about this. Return to Activity 2.1 in this chapter and consider your own family history. If there were moves made by previous generations, it is highly likely they occurred prior to what has been termed 'the global age'. The history of the UK is one of a country of both emigration and immigration. Some of this was by 'choice' while other aspects were based upon 'compulsion'. For example, from the late nineteenth century children were sent to Canada by Dr Barnado for a better life and the Child Migrant Trust uncovered evidence of children still being sent to Australia as late as the 1960s. Earlier still, transportation to the colonies was a punishment much used in the nineteenth century. On the other hand, the UK has always relied upon migrant labour, 'inviting' people to come to the country to undertake low-paid jobs. There are substantial Irish communities, fuelled by the migration of Irish labour during the 1840s onwards; after World War II there was considerable movement of migrant labour from the Caribbean and then from the Indian subcontinent and Africa (notably the arrival of East African Asians after their expulsion from Uganda in the 1970s).

In relation to the movement of capital, enterprises have always sought out cheaper labour, raw materials and new markets; indeed, this drove the expansion of the European empires. The movement of capital in this way, albeit slow, led to migration and settlements over the world, driven by economic imperatives. This also led to a fascination with indigenous cultures, and these have had a consistent impact on art in the 'global North'.

So, the forces that have shaped the current world are a continuation of much of what has gone before. The year 2007 saw the 200th anniversary of the abolition of the slave trade by the British Parliament, a timely reminder not only of Britain's part in such a dehumanising enterprise but also of the contemporary opposition to it. Slavery was arguably a stark manifestation of a globalising impulse based upon exploitation and profit, leaving a few people very rich and many others displaced, impoverished or even dead.

The EU, the local and the global

In our final section we turn to a recent controversy. The expansion of the EU has led to a new form of migration *within* the boundaries of the European Union, which has enshrined the free movement of labour as one of its founding principles (Geyer, 2000). As its boundaries have expanded, the EU has become increasingly restrictive in relation to the position of non-EU nationals, giving rise to the policy of 'Fortress Europe'. Yet this does not prevent thousands of potential migrants from West Africa risking their lives in an attempt to reach Spanish (and therefore EU) territory in the Canary Isles. The expansion of the EU in the early twenty-first century has included many poorer countries from Eastern Europe, and this has seen many of their younger workers move to the established economies of the West. The UK has been a major receiver of much of this low-waged labour. During 2006 many newspapers were full of stories about the 'Polish plumber', skilled tradesmen coming to the UK and filling a gap in the service economy, often at very low rates. At the other end of the market, Eastern Europe has provided a recruiting ground for social work personnel, as those who were trained by UK- and US-influenced programmes in their own countries seek to find better paid employment in the UK, where there is a shortage of social workers (Berry, 2006). Similar trends can be seen in the NHS with recruitment of medical staff from developing countries.

There are clear ethical questions to be asked about this trend: surely highly developed economies should not plunder the skilled workforce from those countries who need them. This is especially relevant in relation to health care professionals, and increasingly so with social work in the UK, which is becoming a more international workforce. There is another side to this question. When considering the economic aspect of migration, governments seem eager to embrace the benefits of the movement of capital and the profits this may bring about. Thus, capital seems largely unrestricted by government, as it seeks to maximise its potential profit. Yet, when an individual decides that there can be a better reward for their skills in the UK, those individuals are subjected to government regulations and hostility from people in the receiving country. One of the features of capitalism, Karl Marx observed, was this very trend: capital knows no borders, and his response was that the working class was also 'international'. This aspect of solidarity among workers has largely disappeared in early twenty-first-century individualism, but for social workers concerned with justice and equality at both local and global levels it is a point to consider.

CHAPTER SUMMARY

In this chapter we have outlined some basic elements of globalisation and demonstrated how these have helped shape local circumstances. These global factors impact upon people's lives, and have always done so. In summary we would suggest that the following are important points for social workers and their educators to consider.

- Our society is made up of many diverse communities with their own histories and these are largely the consequence of global trends and movements in relation to either capital, labour or both.

- Immigration has been a long-standing feature of the UK with movements of people, ideas and skills.

- On one hand this has had positive consequences in the creation of cultural diversity and influence in relation to clothes, food, art and music.

- On the other hand this has also created tensions and misunderstandings, racialised identities, and government controls. All too often this has been accompanied by fear of 'the other' (Brah, 2001) and demonisation of immigrants.

- Global movements are a feature of capitalism and a desire for profit. This is based upon exploitation, which occurs at both global and local levels.

- Social work does not stand apart from the global. It is a local response to a series of difficulties which are influenced by, if not created and sustained by, global factors. Local practice needs to understand this.

FURTHER READING

Adams, A, Erath, P and Shardlow, S (2000) *Fundamentals of social work in selected European Countries.* Lyme Regis: Russell House Publishing. (Chapter 1, pp 1–8).
This chapter introduces the reader to the ways in which social work has been affected by globalisation.

Cousins, M (2005) *European welfare states: Comparative perspectives.* London: Sage. (Chapter 3, pp 41–57).
An easy-to-read section on globalisation with activities to check understanding.

George, V and Wilding, P (2002) *Globalisation and human welfare.* Basingstoke: Palgrave.
This is a good text, quite accessible. Although it is not specific to social work, it does, as the title suggests, deal with questions about human welfare.

Lyons, K, Manion, K and Carlsen, M (2006) *International perspectives on social work: Global conditions and local practice.* Basingstoke: Palgrave Macmillan.
An accessible book with specific chapters on globalisation and migration.

Mishra, R (1999) *Globalisation and the welfare state.* Cheltenham: Edward Elgar Publishing.
This book provides a more comprehensive debate about globalisation, although it is a little more complex.

Non-academic books

Roden, C (2005) *Arabesque: A taste of Morocco, Turkey and Lebanon.* London: Michael Joseph Ltd.
Not just any cookery book, but one which shows how cultures have travelled and borrowed from each other for over 700 years.

Williams, C (2002) *Sugar & slate.* Aberystwyth: Planet.
The account of a second-generation black Briton from North Wales and her searches for identity in Africa, Guyana and Wales.

Chapter 3
Developing an international social work perspective

Karen Lyons and Sue Lawrence

Introduction

The aim of this chapter is to signpost some reflective skills which will help you develop an international perspective and:

- consolidate what you know;

- challenge some of your assumptions;

- develop what you need to know to create an international imagination.

After reflecting briefly on the previous chapters and the nature of international social work, we lay the ground for a fuller discussion of international perspectives in relation to particular user groups discussed in Chapters 4 to 7.

Although international social work can be seen as an area of activity in its own right, it has also been described as *a lens through which to view practice* (Lyons, et al., 2006, p11). In this sense, the essence of an international perspective is based upon social work knowledge, skills and values which are core to the development of all professional practice. However, conditions of globalisation and current trends in demography and migration require us to develop an international perspective. We can do this through increasing our knowledge about comparative welfare and examples of social work practice in other countries and through extending our skills in cross-cultural work. Using an approach which looks at the organisation and/or practices of social work in different countries may constitute 'comparative study' and there has been relatively little research and writing in this field. However, Meeuwisse and Sward (2007) provide a useful analysis of approaches to comparative study and give some examples of studies in particular areas such as child care.

In this book we suggest that there are high degrees of interdependence between individuals and families in one society and another – and between nations themselves. This is evidenced in the way that political, economic and social networks extend beyond national boundaries. This gives rise, on occasion, to the need for transnational social work as we shall illustrate later.

Developing an international perspective requires us to draw on and extend:

- knowledge of social welfare beyond the UK; of different cultures and the different contexts for social work;

- skills in working with people from different countries and minority groups (particularly as these are related to nationality, ethnicity and/or language);

- values which respect difference and promote principles of human rights and social justice.

In this chapter we begin with a brief summary of Chapters 1 and 2 and then suggest how you can use the ideas from those chapters and some new material about the broad context and organisation of social services to develop an international perspective on social work with the service user groups presented in Chapters 4 to 7.

Reflecting on previous chapters and looking ahead

In Chapter 1, we considered some definitions of international social work and how we could make sense of international dimensions, drawing out commonalities and differences to help us reflect upon social work in the UK. The notion of 'journeys' helps us to understand people's life experiences and we discussed diasporas. We also explored what social workers in different countries would have in common, for example, their values and codes of ethics. In Chapter 2 we learned how globalisation as a concept, and global movements of knowledge, people and capital, impact upon all aspects of the social work task. Through this we saw how social workers deal with issues at a local level which may have originated at a global level. We discussed migration, and the challenges arising from the movement of people, as well as the 'push–pull' factors that affect migration patterns. We saw that there are a variety of reasons for decisions to migrate and for the choice of destinations. These are related to economic and political conditions of both the sending and receiving countries, and historical as well as contemporary factors. But we also recognised varying degrees of 'choice' exercised by individuals and families who migrate. People who are smuggled or trafficked have little control over the circumstances of their relocation while asylum seekers are likely to have even less choice in decisions about leaving a country and 'settling' elsewhere (Lyons, et al., 2006). The conditions which people have left – and the circumstances under which people adapt to life in a new country – have implications for the sort of services they need and the skills required of social workers.

We also saw the ways in which globalisation has impacted on the spread of dominant patterns of knowledge and culture (reflecting the economic power of multinational corporations and the political power of particular nations), actually or potentially further disadvantaging particular countries or groups within societies. Within these globalising trends we suggested that, due to its location, various aspects of British policy are affected by membership of the European Union. These influences extend to social and welfare policies and affect our opportunities to learn about and engage with social work in European countries in particular. However, traditionally the UK has had close relationships with Commonwealth and other English-speaking countries and these still have relevance, not least in relation to social work with minorities already settled in the UK and even recruitment of social workers (see Chapter 8).

ACTIVITY 3.1

Think about Chapters 1 and 2 and write down what you believe are the important factors of international social work and how they can affect local practice.

Comment

You might have reflected upon the different definitions of social work internationally, and the way in which an international perspective can assist in viewing local situations and practice. You may also have considered some of the consequences of globalisation:

different forms of migration and their impact; the diversity of local communities; and the international nature of some social problems. You may also have thought about how international social work organisations might be relevant to local situations. These are all themes that will be explored further in later chapters.

Moving on to consider the relevance of international perspectives to social work with different user groups we can note that, whenever we look at social work in countries beyond the UK, social workers usually have responsibilities in relation to a similar range of people. These are primarily people who are vulnerable for some reason, either in the long term or at a particular point in their lives. They may be on the margins of – or even excluded from – mainstream society. This situation may be related to individual characteristics but more often reflects the dominant values, economic chances and presence or absence of equal opportunity policies and anti-oppressive practices in a given society.

In this book we have chosen to focus on the following user groups:

- children, young people and families with problems (Chapter 4);
- people with mental health issues (Chapter 5);
- vulnerable older people (Chapter 6);
- people with disabilities (Chapter 7).

This tends to reflect the way that services are set up in the UK and the user groups to which British social workers most commonly relate; and these groups also tend to be the basis for much social work abroad (although there are also some exceptions). In the following chapters the international dimensions of social work with each user group will be discussed; examples will be given of how social workers in other countries also provide services to these user groups; and the international dimensions of local practice will be indicated.

We shall address some overarching themes, such as:

- commonalities and differences between people and countries;
- social issues and how they are understood and defined in different societies;
- cross-cultural knowledge and communication skills;
- ideas about 'family' and implications for social work;
- values which are inclusive and which advance anti-oppressive practices.

However, in this chapter we will look more closely at some of the contextual and organisational factors which impact upon social work. We start with some information about demographics, that is, the characteristics of the population globally and in different countries. We then look briefly at some of the differences in how social services are organised. This requires us to think more about the role of the state (and alternative ways of providing services) and also about the role of families in different countries. Finally, we shall say something about a generic skill which social workers might increasingly use in multicultural societies and transnational work, that is, working through interpreters.

The relevance of demographics to social work

The form of social work required in different countries is partly determined by the number of people who live in them relative to factors such as gender balance and age distribution in particular societies. Furthermore, the balance between the demand from particular populations and the supply of various resources (including water and agricultural or grazing land; gas and oil) plays a significant part in determining the conditions under which people live. The size of populations and rate of population growth globally and its growth or decline in particular countries also pose challenges for international bodies and for national governments and have implications for economic growth or stability.

The world population in mid 2008 stood at over 6.7 billion people but the number continues to grow at a significant rate (an estimated 1.188 per cent in 2007): for example, the world population increased from only 2 billion in 1930 to 6 billion in 2000 (CIA World Factbook, 2009). Despite relatively recent attempts to curb population growth through its one child policy, China has the largest population at over 1 billion people (1,330,044,544) while nearly 1.5 billion live (at greater density) in the Indian subcontinent. Of these, most live in India (1,147,995,904) relative to smaller numbers (but still high-density concentrations) in Bangladesh (153,546,896) and Pakistan (172,800,048). Countries such as the USA (303,824,640), Brazil (196,342,592), Russia (140,702,096), Japan (127,288,416) and Mexico (109,955,400) have huge populations although the countries are of different sizes (land mass); have varying natural resources; and range from very rich in terms of per capita income (Japan and USA) to not very well off (Russia). However, note that all show huge discrepancies between the richest and poorest sectors of society. In contrast, most countries in the European Union are smaller geographically and demographically, with largest populations in Germany (82,369,552), France (64,057,792) and UK (60,943,912); while many more countries have populations of less than 10 million, for example, Sweden (9,045,389); Ireland (4,156,119) (CIA World Factbook, 2009).

But overall numbers only tell part of the story. Another important aspect is the gender ratio. Worldwide there are 1.01 males to each female, but this ratio varies between countries and also at different stages of the life cycle. For instance, some countries, such as United Arab Emirates and Kuwait, have even higher male to female ratios (2.68 and 1.80 respectively) for the population between 15 and 49 years (figures which may be explained partly by a high proportion of male immigrant workers), while for the age group between birth and 14, countries such as China and India have ratios of 1.13 and 1.10 respectively (US Census Bureau, 2009). In both China and India boy babies tend to be preferred to girls and there are periodic press reports of abandonment, neglect and even infanticide of girl babies. Conversely, in countries where recent civil and cross-border wars have engaged large numbers of the male population, overall gender ratios drop below the norm, such as in Sierra Leone (0.93:1) and the Central African Republic (0.98:1). When the full age range is taken into account, on average 1.07 males are born for every female worldwide, but this figure shifts to an inverse ratio by the time people pass 65 years (0.781 males to each female) (CIA World Factbook, 2009).

The birth rate and age distribution in a given population are also very significant in determining the size of a country's labour force and the proportion of people needing care (at both ends of the age range) relative to those available to take on this role. Overall, 27.3 per cent of the world's population is aged 0–14 years; 65.1 per cent are 15–64 years; and only 7.6 per cent of the population globally is aged 65 years and over (CIA World Factbook, 2009). Traditionally, many less developed countries had a demographic profile in a pyramid shape with a large number of births at the bottom tapering to very few people reaching old age at the top. However, in a number of African countries the AIDS epidemic has altered the shape of the population profile, with a significant decrease in the number of adults fit enough to work or available to care for young and old dependants (Lyons, et al., 2006).

Meanwhile, in many developed countries there are concerns about low birth rates relative to a post-retirement age population which is increasing both in terms of overall numbers and in the length of time that people live beyond national retirement age (commonly 65 years). So, for instance, a recent report stated that Germany now has the lowest birth rate in Europe (8.5 live births per 1,000 inhabitants in 2004), giving rise to concerns about reduced growth, economic decline and an elderly, shrinking population (Harding, 2006). The same report noted that comparative figures for the UK are 12 births per 1,000 and for Ireland 15.2. This figure, in conjunction with age expectancy rates (longevity), gives rise to very different figures for the median age of national populations which ranges from 42.9 years in Japan to as low as 14.8 years in Uganda (United Nations, 2007, Table A 111.5, p66). The term *median age* is a figure which divides the population of a country in two equal halves – with one half being younger than the median age and half being older.

ACTIVITY 3.2

Study the figures given above and suggest some of the reasons why there should be such variations in the median age of the population of different countries. Why should this matter to social workers?

Comment

The above figures indicate that many more people will live to be old in Japan, where 27.9 per cent of the population are over 60 years (UN, 2007) and in many other prosperous countries (including the UK and most other European countries), relative to many developing countries, not least those most affected by AIDS (such as Uganda) where only a small percentage of people survive to 60 years old or beyond. These contrasting situations give rise to differing needs for health and social care provision as well as having implications for pension schemes and other forms of financial aid. Thus, a common concern in many developed countries is the economic cost of an aging population, most particularly a rise in the number of frail elderly people needing either health or social care – or both. The increase in the number of older people in many national populations also challenges publicly held stereotypes as well as requiring changes in the skills and attitudes of social workers and others in the social care workforce (see also Chapter 6).

A final aspect of demographics to note here is the global shift to urbanisation, that is, the proportion of people living in towns and cities, relative to the rural population. Whereas this movement was a feature of the nineteenth century in most countries in 'the West', it is a trend which has increased globally through the twentieth century so that the estimate of the United Nations Population Fund (UNFPA, 2007) that more than half the world's population would be living in cities by 2008 was realised. In 2000 the highest proportions of people living in urban areas were in North America (over 80 per cent), closely followed by Latin America, Europe and Oceania (predominantly Australia and New Zealand). However, the rise in urbanisation is currently most pronounced in Asia and Africa where people migrate in hopes of employment and a better standard of living – but these ambitions may not be realised. While rural areas offer the possibility of subsistence agriculture and community support, the city may be a place of near destitution in shanty towns or on the streets, with people vulnerable to disease (through malnutrition and lack of potable water and sanitation) as well as high rates of crime.

An international perspective on the organisation of social services

One of the points mentioned in Chapter 2 was the extent to which globalising forces may have reduced the power of the state. This is also true if we consider that the UK is now part of a significant regional grouping, that is, the European Union, which has its own Parliament and powers to influence national policies. These points are relevant to social workers since they have led to changes in the welfare state. However, the whole idea of developing a 'welfare state' was particular to some countries in north-west Europe (and to a lesser extent some of the more prosperous Commonwealth countries, such as Canada and New Zealand). There are many countries across the world where social services are primarily provided through the market (the private sector) or the voluntary sector or the informal sector and we shall now look more closely at these variations.

The role of the state in providing social services

The British welfare state was established in the late 1940s following the wartime publication of a major report (the Beveridge Report, 1942) advocating the development of services to counteract the following social problems:

- poverty (Social Security payments);
- poor health (the National Health Service);
- ignorance (universal education);
- idleness (unemployment provisions);
- bad accommodation (low-cost housing).

Wartime experience of the evacuation of children from cities and the effects of separation and some of their foster conditions also led to concerns about protection for children resulting in the establishment of children's departments (one of the services to be combined in local authority social service departments in 1970 and subsequently mainly relocated with education services by 2008).

In fact, some aspects of a welfare state (for example, financial help through social insurance) had been pioneered in Germany in the late nineteenth century. More recently, the welfare state has been most developed – in terms of providing high-quality universal services – in the Nordic countries such as Denmark and Sweden. While creation and maintenance of welfare states are partly a function of the wealth of a country they also reflect political ideals and cultural values which aim for an egalitarian society where 'goods' are shared and the income gap between different groups in society is not extreme. Therefore, a wealthy country such as the USA has not chosen to create a welfare state since the values reflected in political actions have emphasised individual effort and choice, rather than social solidarity.

A significant aspect of the welfare state is the extent to which services are funded and provided by the central state, or perhaps the 'local state', that is, local authorities (in the UK) or 'municipalities' (in many other countries). This is evidenced in the UK in the high proportion of social workers who are employed in the personal social services. For instance, at the turn of the twenty-first century, about 80 per cent of newly qualified social workers were gaining their first employment in social service departments (Lyons and Manion, 2004). An even higher proportion of social workers are employed in municipalities in Denmark and Sweden.

However, by the 1980s and 1990s, the welfare state was coming under attack as being too expensive; creating dependency; and limiting free choice. These criticisms reflected the moves in many countries towards the promotion of the free market economy, itself a feature of globalisation. The result in most countries where a welfare state had flourished was not its total destruction but rather a change in the role of the state. Thus, we see a shift from the state (including the local state) providing all services directly, to the state emphasising its role in planning, regulation and contracting of services. Direct provision of services has become the responsibility of the private and voluntary sectors, resulting in a 'mixed model of welfare' which is now more common in the UK and in many other countries (see, for instance, Carey, 2008).

The role of the private and voluntary sectors

The private and voluntary sectors have a number of distinguishing features, not least that the private sector is profit-orientated while the voluntary sector is sometimes described as the 'not for profit' sector. However, they share common features, such as: they can provide a greater range of services (creating more choice for users); and these may be seen as more responsive to changing social needs and user demand. It is also increasingly the case that agencies in both sectors have to meet minimum standards set by the state and are often contracted to work on behalf of the state.

In the UK the private sector is relatively small overall but plays a significant part in the provision of residential services, particularly for older people. However, this can be contrasted with the situation in the USA where private agencies provide a wide range of 'social services', some of which employ social workers, often in the role of counsellors or therapists. A significant aspect of the private sector is that users are charged directly for services, although in some countries, such as Germany, costs may be reimbursed through insurance schemes. The fee charging element tends to limit the availability of services and to exclude users who lack financial resources. It can thus create actual or perceived differences in the standard of services provided through this sector relative to those provided through statutory or voluntary agencies.

Turning to the voluntary sector, this is sometimes referred to as 'the third sector' and the agencies which provide services were traditionally called charities. (In the UK most voluntary agencies continue to have charitable status.) However, they are now more commonly described as non-governmental organisations (NGOs) or INGOs if they operate at an international level (such as Oxfam or Amnesty International – see Chapter 8). In the UK some NGOs (such as the NSPCC and Barnardo's) had their origins in the nineteenth century (before the state developed social services) and these agencies also gave rise to 'branches' or similar organisations in countries such as Australia and Canada. For the most part, the role of such organisations is relatively small in the UK though they have taken on increased responsibilities for delivering services on behalf of the state since the 1990s and increasing numbers of social workers take up employment in them. While this shift can primarily be seen as a response to global economic and political trends mentioned above, it might also reflect European influence through the idea of subsidiarity. The principle of subsidiarity suggests that decision-making and responsibility should be at the level nearest to the problem, that is, the state should only intervene when the resources of the family or the voluntary sector are insufficient to meet needs. This idea originally derived from the teachings of the Catholic Church and it has for many years been important in shaping social services in some European countries, notably France (Cannan, et al., 1992).

It is apparent therefore that the history and importance of voluntary organisations has been very different in some other European countries. For instance, Germany is an example of a country where, since the late 1940s, social services have mainly been provided through the voluntary sector. There seem to be two reasons for this. Lorenz (1994) identified fear of the power of the central state following the rise of the Nazi movement in the 1930s and the misuse of social services during the Second World War. At the same time, in the period following the war, the Americans played a very significant role in the reconstruction of Europe, including Germany, and favoured social services delivered through the voluntary sector rather than the state. However, this was also consistent with the cultural values of the German population (traditionally divided fairly evenly between Catholics and Protestants) who would favour the principle of subsidiarity.

A national case example

There are now a wide range of voluntary agencies in Germany, varying in size and the type of services provided. Many receive funding from the central state or municipalities and employ social workers. However, there are a few major providers, sometimes referred to as 'the big six' as follows:

- *Deutscher Caritasverband* (Catholic welfare organisation);
- *Diakonisches Werk der Evangelischen Kirche in Deutschland* (Protestant);
- *Zentrale Wolfahrtstelle der Juden in Deutschland* (Jewish welfare);
- *Arbeiterwohlfahrt* (workers' welfare);

- *Deutscher Paritaetischer Wolfahrtsverband* (non-denominational, non-political umbrella organisation).
- *Deutsches Rotes Kreuz* (German Red Cross).

(Cannan, et al., 1992, pp53–4).

While a number of the organisations listed above have religious origins and affiliations, the provision of services is not necessarily restricted to their own followers since there are usually local arrangements to ensure that social services are available to anyone who needs them on a local basis. We can also note here that some of the above organisations operate in a number of countries, not just Germany, as will be discussed further in Chapter 8.

The role of the informal sector

This sector covers a range of actual or potential helpers and carers from within the nuclear or extended family through to friends and neighbours. It also extends to unfunded and strictly voluntary community groups, such as neighbourhood associations and organised youth groups. By definition, social workers are not normally 'employed' in this sector but it is clearly important for social workers to know about family and community resources and to work in harmony with them, particularly when community development, rather than individual treatment, is the main focus of professional intervention.

This was historically an important sector for provision of basic social services in all countries only just over a century ago and continues to be so in many less developed countries, today. This is partly because some states (for example, the Ukraine) do not have the money to invest in substantial public welfare services, and perhaps not even to subsidise the activities of NGOs. However, it is also important in terms of cultural views about the role of the (extended) family and/or the wider community. For instance, in societies where Confucian values are dominant (e.g. China) shame can be felt in talking about problems (which may be to do with children's behaviour, mental health issues, or marital relations) outside the family.

In societies with well-developed social services there have also been assumptions for some time that some minority ethnic groups prefer to meet the needs of their own members rather than turn to 'the authorities' or professionals from the dominant/majority population. This may be the case when new groups arrive and settle in an area: there may be language limitations in terms of accessing services and they may prefer help from people who have had similar experiences and share similar cultural values. However, it has also given rise, for instance in the UK and USA, to debates about how far services have been developed to meet the diversity of ethnic needs in a given locality and how best to train social workers in 'cultural competence'.

The need to recognise the resources of the family and community and to intervene in ways which support and enhance the informal sector has also achieved greater prominence in the shift to the mixed economy of welfare. One such example in the UK was the establishment of Sure Start in the late 1990s. This was initially intended to build on the activities of local community groups in supporting the efforts of parents caring for preschool children in deprived areas. While this can be interpreted as a cynical move to cut the costs of providing preventive services and care for millions of vulnerable members of society, it might also be seen as a way of empowering individuals and communities and valuing the strengths which they possess. Clearly, a mixed economy of care must include the informal sector and this requires professionals to extend their skills and employ group and community work approaches; approaches which tend to be more widely taught on social work courses in European countries other than the UK.

The changing role and form of families

We referred above to the role of the family in providing basic services to its members. This is a theme that will be returned to in the following chapters in relation to specific user groups. However, given the universality of this smallest unit of social organisation, it is important to say more here about the form and function of families. These have been changing over time and also show differences when examined from an international perspective. Indeed, it is more appropriate to refer to 'families', rather than 'the family', since a significant change has occurred in the range of family forms now evident in many societies.

In earlier sociological writing about 'the family' a distinction was made between the nuclear family – a father, mother and 2.4 children in many Western societies – and the extended family. The latter often consisted of three generations and perhaps also unmarried aunts and uncles or cousins sharing a home. This form can still be found in many less developed countries and also in some quite wealthy ones, such as Thailand. Such extended families were able to meet a wide range of the family's practical, social and emotional needs: they usually provided constraints and opportunities for individual family members and, collectively, extended families contributed to creating stable societies in which people felt secure.

This form is less commonly seen in Westernised countries now than it would have been a century ago, although sharing of households, particularly between generations, may be found in some minority ethnic communities, either through choice or economic circumstances. It has also been argued that some families have retained (or recovered) some aspects of the practical and emotional support functions of families (for instance, child care being shared with grandparents or between sisters) even though they are less likely to be living in the same house. It is also possible that more families are being drawn into accommodating and caring directly for family members who are older or who have a physical or mental disability than previously, due to the shift to 'community care' (see Chapters 5, 6 and 7).

However, when speaking of care for children or vulnerable adult relatives, it is important to acknowledge that we are generally (though not exclusively) talking about care by a female relation – most often a mother, sister or daughter. This is significant given the substantial changes which have taken place in the role and expectations of women. Traditionally (and still in many societies), women performed functions in the home and even single women were constrained in terms of the opportunities for education and employment open to them – a factor which had a bearing even on the origins of social work itself. However, during the Second World War, women in the UK and many other countries formed an important part of the labour force. After a relatively brief period when they returned to their domestic roles, the 1960s saw the origins of women's liberation in the USA, UK and elsewhere.

This movement had a number of aspects and consequences. These included the attitudinal changes of women themselves and demands for equal treatment, notably in the spheres of education and employment, which ultimately resulted in legislative change in many societies. This social movement went alongside scientific/medical advances: arguably the most significant of these was the introduction of the contraceptive pill, giving many women reliable control over their reproductive functions for the first time ever (and, incidentally, probably making a significant contribution to the fall in birth rates in many developed countries which we noted earlier in this chapter).

Increasing numbers of women entered – and stayed in – the workforce, a trend which was partly necessitated as standards and costs of living rose. This was not least in countries such as Sweden and Finland where high-quality welfare provisions demand high rates of taxation. However, in these countries relatively generous provisions regarding parental leave (that is, both maternity and paternity leave) have been established as well as high-quality nurseries and after-school facilities for children.

Elsewhere, in most of the countries of the former Soviet Union (FSU), equal opportunities between the sexes had long been espoused (at least in terms of expectations about working) and public day care for children under school age was the norm. This situation was drastically reversed with the break-up of the Soviet Union from 1989. Many families were plunged into poverty because work opportunities in traditional industries dried up and public services (such as nurseries) were closed as newly formed national governments (e.g. in countries such as Lithuania) started on the drive to privatisation in their efforts to join the world (capitalist) economy.

Another change in family forms, sometimes attributed to women's emancipation and then later to the rights which gay men and lesbian women claimed for themselves, was an increase in the number of lone-parent families (usually headed by women) or families where both parents were women (or, more occasionally, men). Both these changes have been seen as problematic – either by policy-makers, concerned about how lone-parent families can be supported, or by groups within society (sometimes religiously based) which view any deviation from children having two parents of the opposite sex as either immoral or simply 'bad for children'. Of course, there are complex arguments which can be advanced by people holding different positions to support their views, but the reality is that most Western societies now accept a variety of family forms which do not accord with the idealised image of nuclear families assumed to be the norm in Britain and America a generation ago.

These changes have implications for how we organise social services and also for the role of social workers themselves. In the first place, although the trend has been to expect more from women in the direct care of vulnerable relatives, in many countries, including Germany and France, fewer women are available (or willing) to take on such care. In the second case, social workers who might previously have found themselves involved with families where there were marital or child-rearing problems in a nuclear family are more likely to find themselves supporting a woman in leaving an abusive relationship – or surviving as a lone parent.

Additionally, although marital breakdown has increased, the number of people who expect to live in a stable relationship with another adult (if not to remarry) is considerable and many children find themselves in 'reconstituted families' where relationships with step-parents (and perhaps step- or half-siblings) may be harmonious – or may prove to be problematic. Such changes have also provided social workers in the areas of adoption and fostering with new challenges, as social workers in different societies argue the case for placement of some children with a lone parent or same sex parents, who do not conform to the traditional idea of a substitute family assumed to be necessary for such placements.

But the emancipation of women has not been a universal phenomenon, as has been illustrated in an edited book about men and masculinity in a global world (Pease and Pringle, 2001). Specific chapters provide examples of societies, predominantly in Africa, Asia and South America, where paternalistic attitudes and behaviours persist, limiting women's opportunities and sometimes more fundamentally affecting the economic position of families and even the gender balance in society, as noted above. In relation to China, the one-child policy and preference for boy babies (mentioned above) has since resulted in reports of whole villages where young men in their twenties have virtually no chance of finding a wife; of obesity and selfish behaviour as a consequence of 'only children' being spoilt; and of girl children needing residential care in orphanages or being available in disproportionate numbers for adoption, including by overseas adopters.

Differences in attitudes to the family, the authority of fathers, and the roles of women, sometimes also prove problematic when minority ethnic groups from traditional societies settle in the West. In countries like the UK the expectations about the 'free and easy' relationships which young men and women establish can clash with the norms of families, for instance from Pakistan or Somalia, and can result in individual unhappiness, family conflict, and families feeling shamed or dishonoured. This in turn can lead to young people being returned to their country of origin for a 'forced marriage' or even occasionally to be the subject of so-called 'honour killings'. Such events clearly confront social workers with challenges to understand the dynamics and respect the norms of families which seem very different from their own, but also to protect the individual rights of young people who may need protection by someone outside the immediate family. It also requires the establishment of trusted relationships with relevant community leaders who may be in a position to offer cultural mediation. This brings us on to considering the skills which might be needed in working cross-culturally, or even in some cases transnationally, and in this chapter we will focus on language differences and the skill of working through interpreters.

Summarising the last two sections we can note the following points.

- There are significant differences between the role of the state and the voluntary sector even between developed countries, such as in Denmark or Germany.

- In the USA a far higher proportion of social workers are 'self-employed' or work in private organisations relative to the UK. Additionally, there is an international shift towards provision of social services by private agencies, some of which are multinational corporations.

- Informal care is the norm in many less developed countries of the global South and was more important in countries such as Greece and Spain until recently.

- In Northern countries family structures are now more varied – and care of children and vulnerable adult relations by (female) family members may conflict with the changed role and increased employment of women.

Working through interpreters

This chapter has mainly provided an international perspective on demography; the various ways in which social services are organised; and different ideas about 'the family'. However, the theme of migration has never been far from the surface and current migration patterns require all social workers to develop skills in working cross-culturally. We also suggest that some local social workers will find themselves working 'transnationally', as extended families settle in different countries, or, for instance, as childless couples look beyond their own shores to adopt babies.

CASE STUDY

A woman from Eastern Europe who had migrated to Israel with her husband subsequently divorced him and came to England with her new husband (a citizen of a European Union country) bringing her son from her first marriage. She then approached a London social services department wishing to make arrangements for the boy to be adopted by her new husband. The social worker needed to get the agreement of the boy's father to this arrangement and initially conducted a telephone interview working through an interpreter. When the father was reluctant to agree, the social worker requested assistance from the agency, International Social Services, which would arrange for a local social worker to visit the father in Israel.

This example indicates that one aspect of working with people from minority ethnic communities or becoming involved in cross-border social work, in terms of skills development, is the ability to work through interpreters. Sanders (2003) has suggested that ... *linguistic minorities are disadvantaged in terms of the level and quality of care they receive, while service providers are compromised in their professional duties* (p74). She and others have made it clear that the use of children or other clients from the same community is not to be recommended. Their use is inappropriate, raising issues of understanding, confidentiality, conflicts of interest and power dynamics. It is therefore important to access appropriately trained community or public service interpreters whenever possible, since such people need familiarity with the social work context and clarity about their own role as well as relevant cultural understanding. When working through an interpreter there is a need to clarify expectations and establish working relationships both between the two professionals and with the service user: what was typically a two-way relationship becomes a tripartite communication process.

Sanders (2003) identifies three models of interpreting. In the Linguistic model *(p76) the interpreter is a language conduit ... enabling communication through accurate interpreting.... He or she may be a freelance interpreter who can provide technical precision, language skills and neutrality. Such a model is sufficient when the service user is articulate, has some understanding about the service on offer and the purpose of the interview is clear, but there are potential gaps related to culture and power which may render this model unsuitable in some situations. Interviews by telephone using an interpreter is a variation of this model (p77) and in the UK there is a particular agency used by social service departments to locate someone who speaks the required language.*

Secondly, Sanders describes the Professional Team model. *In some situations, interpreting is such a regular requirement that one member of a team is an interpreter, acting as a* link worker *between the service provider and a particular community. For example, in Belgium* intercultural mediators *are employed in health-based service teams. One possible disadvantage of this model is that, although interpreters will have taken a course and gained a relevant qualification, they may not be as well regarded as staff qualified to undertake the core work of the agency, or conversely, such people – who often have their origins in a local minority ethnic group – may lose the trust of that community since they are now employed by 'the authorities' (pp77–8).*

It seems likely that, in many cases, the third model described by Sanders is the most compatible with social work, that is, the Client centred or Advocacy model. *In this case bilingual community workers, employed by a community-based organisation, represent the views of service users. In this sense the interpreters are often undertaking an advocacy role in which they need knowledge of services, rights and resources as well as a professional relationship with the service user. They need to have established the expectations and needs of individual service users to adequately represent them but they may also take up more widespread issues on behalf of the whole community (pp78–9).*

Sanders suggests some practical steps which can be taken when carrying out interviews through an interpreter and warns about the need for adequate preparation, including through three-way discussion to clarify roles and expectations.
Suggested steps are as follows.

- Define the purpose of the interview.

- Allow extra time (double the normal interview time).

- Give an indication of how long a session will take.

- Ensure that service user and interpreter can use the same language or dialect (for example, Arabic is ranked sixth among world languages but there are wide variations in how it is spoken in different countries of the Middle East; India is home to many different languages – so simply knowing that someone is 'Indian' does not imply a particular language).

- Match gender of client and interpreter if possible.

- Think about the possible implications of age differences if these are likely to be significant.

- Be aware of possible political, cultural or religious differences, even when people apparently speak the same language.

- Consider possible conflicts of interests.

- Beware of false assumptions (in relation to either the interpreter or the service user).

In fact, many of these 'steps' echo concerns or considerations we might have when carrying out cross-cultural work, whether or not there is a language difference as well. But the crucial difference is the dynamic introduced when two people communicate through a third person, a process which even quite experienced social workers have initially found unsettling and deskilling. However, allowing time for discussion between the social worker and interpreter before the interview, as well as a debriefing session after, should enable both parties to establish an appropriate role-relationship which will work to the advantage, rather than disadvantage, of the service user. (For further discussion of this issue see also Tribe and Raval, 2002.) On a final note, Lucock, et al. (2006) have identified that as yet there is … *no empirical research on how social workers and children might communicate effectively through interpreters* (p29) but, clearly, it is sometimes as necessary to draw on the skills of an interpreter when working with children as with adults and some of the steps outlined above would apply.

C H A P T E R   S U M M A R Y

After a brief discussion of the international and local demographic contexts within which social workers operate, this chapter has raised a number of points, including the need for:

- all social workers to adopt international perspectives in order to engage effectively with the potential range of people seeking services;

- international and comparative knowledge in relation to demographic trends and national variations, to develop appropriate forms of social work and community development;

- social workers to have some knowledge about differences internationally in a) how services are organised and b) norms and expectations of families, since both of these have implications for the practice of social workers.

In addition it is suggested that many social workers will become involved in cross-cultural work and some may be involved in transnational work, even when operating as locally based social workers. This raises the possibility that social workers need to develop skill in working through an interpreter, in addition to cultural competence.

ACTIVITY 3.3

Returning to two case studies first presented in Chapter 1, imagine that the following may have occurred:

Ali is a young man who has arrived from Iraq, he has fled torture and the loss of his family. A social worker has been asked to interview Ali to ascertain his needs and background details as he is claiming he is 15 years old and as such is an unaccompanied minor. The translator who has been sent to work with you says she does not fully understand the young man's dialect and as an aside says she thinks he looks much older than 15. The social worker says they should proceed with the interview and that between them they should be able to communicate sufficiently to establish the basic details.

Portia came to your country from the Caribbean and has lived there for the past 60 years. She was looked after in the Caribbean by her grandmother before joining her parents when she was 15 years old. She had expected to return home in her old age but she no longer has roots there. The social worker interviewing Portia to comprehensively assess her needs prior to a hospital discharge dismisses Portia's comments about returning home, saying that she lived there a long time ago and she is clearly not well enough to travel such a long way. The social worker suggests they should think about Portia's immediate needs and how best to meet them.

Reflecting on what you have read in the previous chapters, list suggestions about how these two cases might have been approached using an international perspective, and what sort of resources should have been put in place, or other types of agency that might have helped.

FURTHER READING

Littlechild, B, Erath, P and Keller, J (eds) (2005) *De- and reconstruction in European social work.* Stassfurt: ISIS.

Although focusing only on Europe, this edited book firstly presents five theoretical chapters which discuss different welfare regimes and implications for social workers of recent political changes and current social trends. In the second part authors present information and ideas about welfare systems and social work in selected European countries (Finland, Norway, Spain, England, Germany, Netherlands and France).

Chapter 4

International aspects of social work with children, young people and families

Graeme Simpson and Brian Littlechild

ACHIEVING A SOCIAL WORK DEGREE

This chapter will enable you to become familiar with the following National Occupational Standards for Social Work.

Key Role 1: Prepare for, and work with individuals, families, carers, groups and communities to assess their needs and circumstances.

3.1 Assess and review the preferred options of individuals, families, carers, groups and communities

3.2 Assess needs, risks and options taking into account legal and other requirements

3.3 Assess and recommend an appropriate course of action for individuals, families, carers, groups and communities

Key Role 3: Support individuals to represent their needs, views and circumstances.

10.3 Advocate for, and with, individuals, families, carers, groups and communities

Key Role 4: Manage risk to individuals, families, carers, groups, communities, self and colleagues.

12.1 Identify and assess the nature of the risk

Key Role 6: Demonstrate professional competence in social work practice.

19.3 Work within the principles and values underpinning social work practice

20.1 Identify and assess issues, dilemmas and conflicts that might affect your practice

It will also introduce you to the following academic standards set out in the Quality Assurance Agency social work subject benchmark statement.

5.1.1 Social work services, service users and carers.

- the social processes (associated with, for example, poverty, migration, unemployment, poor health, disablement, lack of education and other sources of disadvantage) that lead to marginalisation, isolation and exclusion, and their impact on the demand for social work services;
- explanations of the links between definitional processes contributing to social differences (for example, social class, gender, ethnic differences, age, sexuality and religious belief) and the problems of inequality and differential need faced by service users;
- the nature of social work services in a diverse society (with particular reference to concepts such as prejudice, interpersonal, institutional and structural discrimination, empowerment and anti-discriminatory practices);
- the nature and validity of different definitions of, and explanations for, the characteristics and circumstances of service users and the services required by them, drawing on knowledge from research, practice experience, and from service users and carers;

- the focus on outcomes, such as promoting the well-being of young people and their families, and promoting dignity, choice and independence for adults receiving services.

5.1.2 The service delivery context.

- the location of contemporary social work within historical, comparative and global perspectives, including European and international contexts;
- the changing demography and cultures of communities in which social workers will be practising;
- the complex relationships between public, social and political philosophies, policies and priorities and the organisation and practice of social work, including the contested nature of these.

5.1.3 Values and ethics.

- aspects of philosophical ethics relevant to the understanding and resolution of value dilemmas and conflicts in both interpersonal and professional contexts.

5.1.4 Social work theory.

- the relevance of sociological perspectives to understanding societal and structural influences on human behaviour at individual, group and community levels;
- the relevance of psychological, physical and physiological perspectives to understanding personal and social development and functioning;
- models and methods of assessment, including factors underpinning the selection and testing of relevant information, the nature of professional judgement and the processes of risk assessment and decision-making;

5.1.5 The nature of social work practice.

- the place of theoretical perspectives and evidence from international research in assessment and decision-making processes in social work practice;
- the integration of theoretical perspectives and evidence from international research into the design and implementation of effective social work intervention, with a wide range of service users, carers and others.

Introduction

Earlier chapters have set out general reasons for you to engage with 'International perspectives'. In this chapter we want to identify the reasons why you need to do this in relation to children, young people, their families and carers before discussing some of the areas where children's global experiences have a direct impact upon local practice. The United Kingdom is a country which has a lengthy history of migration and movement of people (see Chapter 2). When families move around they bring with them their own traditions and customs, their religious faiths and ways of bringing up their children. Adjusting to a new set of traditions and child-rearing 'norms' creates difficulties for families and this is something social workers need to develop an awareness of and sensitivity to. For the families, however, these experiences are often made worse by discrimination and isolation in the UK. Many migrants experience a sense of loss for the country they have left, even if the migration has resulted from positive choices and experiences. Such experiences are often compounded by the effects of trauma and grief, as they flee war-torn countries (Richman, 1998; Huegler, 2005). Discrimination also affects children and families who have migrated to the UK, even when those families have been settled for many generations.

These are themes that we will develop in the chapter as we demonstrate the importance of adopting an international perspective in this area for your current UK practice. We will begin, however, by briefly exploring what is meant by 'childhood'.

Think about what it means to be a child. What do we mean by childhood *and what does a* good childhood *consist of?*

Comment

Your responses to this activity should have begun to draw on the material in the introduction. A cursory reading of daily newspapers, listening to or viewing the evening news should have alerted you to the fact that 'childhood' will inevitably differ according to where the child lives. So, for many children in Sierra Leone, for example, childhood in recent years was characterised by exposure to war, in contrast to children living in the UK during the same period. Diane Gittens (1997) argued that childhood is socially constructed. By that she means that the nature of the society that a child grows up in, the demands placed upon the child in that society and how the child is viewed and treated by adults will be 'constructed', that is determined, by social factors. She identified that childhood is constructed according to time, place and gender. To put this simply, the experiences of children in any given society will differ across generations (we expect that your parents or grandparents will have experienced a different type of childhood to you). They will also differ from place to place; thus, as we will read later in this chapter, the experiences of children in Africa or Asia are quite different from the experiences of children in Western Europe. Finally, Gittens draws our attention to the fact that childhood experiences will be different for girls and boys. To this we can also add that the way society responds to children will affect their experience, for example in relation to how children who commit offences are viewed and dealt with, or how child abuse is responded to differently in Europe (Hetherington, et al., 1997).

There is another factor that we need to consider here and that is, at what point does childhood end? This is sufficiently difficult to grasp with reference only to contemporary UK society – just think about the anomalies in legislation – but it becomes even more complex when international perspectives are considered. For example, in some societies children under ten years old are routinely engaged in working, whereas in others this is not the case.

Once you have come to some conclusions about what childhood actually is, consider the question, What do children have a right to and need? *Who do you think should be satisfying these needs – parents, extended family, or social work agencies?*

Comment

We would expect many and varied answers here, probably beginning with very basic items, for example, food, shelter and clothing, as envisaged in Maslow's hierarchy of needs (1954). Others would focus upon positive relationships between children and their parents or caregivers; or a safe and secure environment for the child to grow up in, to develop the child's full potential; health care being available; or, the provision of education for the child. Thus, a full range of needs can be identified, each one of which we would suggest most people living in the UK would regard as a child's fundamental 'right'. Many of the factors necessary to satisfy these needs would be provided by parents, carers or 'family'. This leads on to the question, what should a child expect from the state or social work agencies? We have already established in earlier chapters that, internationally, 'social work' is a broad concept. General health care, education, good opportunities for development would all, in some countries, be seen as part of broad 'social work' provision, but we imagine that most people reading this book would have identified what social workers in their country actually do. For the UK, many of you would have thought about the Government policy *Every Child Matters* (ECM) (HM Government, 2003).

After the Lord Laming Inquiry into the death of Victoria Climbié, a child originally from West Africa, the UK Government undertook a comprehensive review into the full range of child care services and produced a raft of policy documents which sought to integrate all children's services in England. There are five broad aims:

- be healthy;
- stay safe;
- enjoy and achieve;
- make a positive contribution;
- achieve economic well-being.

One of the ways in which this policy helps shape our views about children is that it sees them as being a 'future investment' and having clear 'welfare needs'. Society spends money to promote child welfare because, in everyday language, it will be 'money well spent'. You may not necessarily see children in this way; other aspects of 'childhood' are that it is a time of 'innocence' and 'dependency', while others see children as full people with their own rights (Franklin, 2002).

Franklin writes about children's rights and suggests there are two basic sets of rights: autonomy and the right to welfare. These are emphasised in the United Nations Convention on the Rights of the Child (UNCRC, 1989), which the UK signed in 1991. The UNCRC is accepted worldwide and by 1995 it had been signed by 177 countries, though notably the USA and Somalia have yet to sign. You should read the 54 articles and protocols of the Convention in full (www.unicef.org/crc/), but we will draw your attention to article two, which is especially relevant for this chapter. This article states that children should not experience *discrimination of any kind, irrespective of the child's or his or her parents' or legal guardians' race, colour, sex, language, religion, political or other opinion, national, ethnic or social origin, property, disability, birth or other status* and that this extends to the child's parents and family. The article also states that children's rights should not be restricted because of their legal status. You will also find that these basic principles are inherent in social work's ethical principles and codes.

You should now read the British Association of Social Workers (2002) *and* International Federation of Social Workers *(2004) ethical principles and codes (see website addresses in the References section at the end of this book).*

Make a note of these points, and as you read through the following sections think about the extent to which they can be applied to the groups of children we discuss in the light of Every Child Matters.

Seeking health and safety: Refugees and asylum-seeking childen

We begin with a small case study, reported by Paul Lewis in *The Guardian* newspaper in May 2007. The report highlights the experience of two teenage boys who were living in Birmingham, having been smuggled out of Afghanistan as stowaways in lorries, sometimes clinging to the undercarriage, and brought to England. They witnessed deaths and other forms of violence, before being left in Birmingham. As you read through it, consider how social workers should work with the boys.

CASE STUDY

An Afghan community worker in Birmingham interviewed in The Guardian *(Lewis, 2007) says that many asylum-seeking Afghan boys have approached him seeking help. He says that, in his experience, the local social service department often gives young people 'artificial' ages and fails to care for them appropriately. As a result, the community worker is concerned about the young people's welfare:* How can these children know how to change a light bulb, use electricity or cook? It is dangerous leaving them alone in these houses. *A particular concern for him is the mental health of Afghan refugee boys, many of whom have witnessed the death of people who travelled with them to the UK as 'stowaways'.*

Ramazan and Abdul-Khaliq, two Afghan boys interviewed in the same article, talk about the haunting nightmares they experience in relation to their journeys to the UK. Ramazan was separated from his family while they were crossing a border with hundreds of other refugees during the night, on foot through rough mountain terrain. I was shouting, calling their names, *he says.* Whenever I asked the smuggler [to help] he said be quiet, I will take you to your parents. I was crying. Some of them [fellow travellers or agents] were laughing. Others said, 'don't worry; we will take you to your parents. *Arriving in the UK and seeing the grey tarmac and tall buildings of Birmingham, Ramazan remembers that he knew that he must have arrived at his final destination, because there were no more lorries to climb into. He found himself totally alone.* I have asked people to help find my family, but no one has helped.

Adapted from *The sorry plight of the refugee children* by Paul Lewis, *The Guardian*, 24 May 2007

Comment

The experience of childhood is one which is quite different from that experienced by most children born in England. The *Every Child Matters* principles of being healthy and safe are ones which these children and their families risked their lives to find. To return to our earlier question, then, what should these children expect from parents or social work agencies? The parents tried to get their children to a 'safe haven', the UK, by whatever means they could, and some died in the attempt. When in the UK, these two children were assumed to be older than they actually were by social workers. Crawley (2006) notes that disputes over a child's age are commonplace. In 2004, the first year for which statistics for unaccompanied asylum seekers were available, 44 per cent of applicants were *age disputed and treated as adults* (Crawley, 2006, p16). She suggests that increasingly social workers have to play a regulatory role which clearly does not fit easily with the British Association of Social Workers' Code of Ethics, let alone international codes. Cemlyn and Briskman (2003) argue that asylum-seeking children often have their basic human rights ignored by the agencies who should be promoting them. Some refugee children are escaping countries where there are conflicts, like the two boys in the case study. Other refugee children have not only lived in a war-torn country, but have been actively involved in the conflict as child soldiers.

Child soldiers, rehabilitation and social work

The United Nations estimate that there are over 250,000 children presently fighting in wars, most of them in Africa. At a conference in February 2007, held in Paris, a number of countries signed a commitment to *Free Children from War* (UNICEF, 2007a). UNICEF reported on the situation in the Central African Republic, where it is estimated that around 50 per cent of children attend school, falling to 14 per cent in the war zones, and where malnutrition affects about 40 per cent of the child population. Many children are left with little alternative but to join military forces, since this becomes a means of survival (Chevigny, 2007). Høiskar (2001) reviews the research into child soldiers and identifies poverty as a constant factor which was present in the experiences of children who became child soldiers. Poor families were less likely to be able to fund any escape for their children, but children frequently volunteer as a means of securing food and shelter. The Paris meeting has had the effect of several countries taking immediate steps to address this question. In the Central African Republic a programme of supported demobilisation has been established focusing upon health care, education, protection, security and recreation activities (Chevigny, 2007). The emphasis is upon trying to reunite children with their families and ensure that there is a strong network of community-based supports. Zack-Williams (2006) writes about the need for rehabilitation programmes in Africa to develop methods which build upon the strengths of indigenous people and ideas, and to avoid simply adapting paradigms from Europe and America. He cites Gbla (2003), who noted that in Sierra Leone, after the war, there was only one psychiatrist to undertake any psychosocial work, but that in any event, traditional African beliefs would seek out a community-based form of rehabilitation and not an individualised one. While not ruling out therapeutic interventions, Zack-Williams argues for a community-based approach to rehabilitation grounded in indigenous approaches, which poses a significant challenge to international social work and non-governmental organisations. His concluding comments, however, move the discussion to practice in Europe, where the presence of a considerable number of refugee and asylum-seeking children, who have experienced life as child soldiers, needs to be addressed. This underlines one of the themes of this book: international social work is not just 'global' but is also very 'local'.

RESEARCH SUMMARY

Ravi Kohli (2006) conducted a small research study into how social workers in England respond to unaccompanied refugee and asylum-seeking children. He found that many children watched how those who hear their stories responded to them. Many of the children either remained silent or gave scant information about their previous lives, behaving as if they were a 'closed book'. Kohli suggests that refugee children are very resilient, but that their reluctance to speak about their past is interpreted as a fear of speaking about the unimaginable. He argues that not speaking about situations is part of an ordinary adolescence, and should be seen as part of growing up. Kohli cites Papadopoulos (2002) who argues that for many refugees silence is in fact a deliberate part of the healing process. Kohli writes that previous bad experiences of authority figures lead, for many children, to a mistrust of the authorities in England. He categorises social workers' descriptions of the experiences and responses of children as follows:

- *children who were too shocked to talk;*

- *those who had been told to keep quiet, because their families could be put at risk;*

- *children who, despite all they had experienced, just wanted to get on with life;*

- *children who were so uncertain about the future they were not able to reflect on the past.*

The social workers in Kohli's study described four ways in which children communicated about how they came to be in England:

- *those children who knew what was happening and spoke openly about it;*

- *those who knew but would not say;*

- *those who did not know what was happening and were open about their bewilderment;*

- *those who did not appear to know why they had been sent by families and who maintained a confused silence.*

The response of social workers fell into three categories:

- *those social workers who were sceptical but acted as practical helpers;*

- *those who offered the children help with understanding and provided a form of help which was therapeutic;*

- *those who befriended the children in the best interests of the child, whatever the response of the authorities.*

Asylum seekers and refugees: Enjoy, achieve and make a positive contribution?

Kohli's research has been summarised here in some detail because it provides important information for social workers who will be working with unaccompanied refugee and asylum-seeking children. He does not offer any view of which response is preferable and says that many social workers become sceptical because they have heard similar stories many times before. This does not diminish the validity of the stories.

The research summary above draws our attention to how social workers respond to the children and we have placed this in the context of two other *ECM* objectives. If refugee children are to enjoy, achieve and make positive contributions then it is essential that they receive good initial services from social workers. In his article in *The Guardian* (see the Case Study above), Lewis (2007) writes that refugee children often look older because of what they have experienced. He also mentions two refugee boys who comment upon the laughter and enjoyment of other 13-year-olds in Birmingham returning from school, by saying: *That is what other 13-year-olds are like in this country.* This statement indicates that the experiences of refugee children contrast with those of other children living in the UK. Many local authorities have developed strong policies to assist with the education of refugee children. In 2003, the Refugee Council estimated that there were over 99,000 refugee children in UK schools concentrated in London Boroughs, Manchester, Birmingham and Glasgow (Bolloten and Spafford, 2005). Integrated children's services mean that this is an area where social workers need to develop their knowledge and expertise, especially since the Home Office operates a policy of dispersal; that is, sending asylum seekers and refugees to different parts of the country. Finally, read the following short research summary about the experiences of young separated refugees.

RESEARCH SUMMARY

Huegler (2005) examined the research evidence, and carried out empirical research, into the experiences of young separated refugees aged 16 and 17, in both Germany and the United Kingdom. She found that while in the United Kingdom (as compared to Germany) more children were supported within the child welfare system, there were concerns that responses were influenced by costs rather than needs-led care, with a lack of appropriate planning and monitoring. On a more general European level, Huegler noted the concerns of a number of commentators that the protection of refugees is based on the 'lowest common denominator' among European Union member states, reflecting a wider move that attempts to discourage refugees from seeking asylum in Europe. Social workers supporting young separated refugees need to take such broader political contexts into account in their work with these children.

Much more can be written about refugee children and they are a continual reminder of how the 'global' and the 'local' intersect. At the end of the book, we have included some useful web-based resources for you to follow up.

Child Labour: Achieving economic well-being?

Zack-Williams (2006, p124) makes the link between the issues of child soldiers and child labour, where at very young ages children cease to become *a liability, dependent upon the family, instead they soon become an asset as a source of income to the family*. It is likely that some children who arrive in this country from overseas may have been child workers and may have made vital contributions to the family income. Thus, childhood will have quite different meanings for these children and their families.

ACTIVITY 4.4

Think about your own childhood. When did you start to 'work'? What type of work was it? Was the work paid or unpaid? Was it for an employer or in the family business?

The work that children can undertake in the UK is quite limited by legislation that has been developed over the past 185 years. No doubt your experience of work will be largely determined by where and when you grew up, confirming Gittens's (1997) view that childhood is constructed over time and place. In the UK during the 1930s, it was commonplace for children to start work at 14; earlier still children began work at 12; the grandfather of one of the authors of this chapter was working on a farm at the age of six and never went to school. Times may have changed in the UK, but for children in other parts of the world, paid work is part of their daily routine. The extent of child labour worldwide is well documented, but it is also something which is inextricably linked with life in the rich 'Northern' countries. Child labour helps produce cheap goods which are bought in the UK and Western Europe, and UK consumers, including social welfare professionals, benefit, even if it is unwittingly, from this trend. The International Labour Organisation (ILO) reported that in 2006 one in seven children was engaged in work on a regular basis, many for very low wages (ILO, 2006). In the UK, the minimum wage does not apply until the age of 21 (Price and Simpson, 2007, p92). Child labour, however, is not straightforward and Lyons et al. (2006, pp147–9) identify three different aspects of child labour, which can be:

1. *An educational or empowering tool – providing that employment is separated from exploitation it can bring about a form of education and even career planning.*

2. *A survival mechanism – this is not merely referring to the fact that in many countries children contribute to the family income and without this labour the family would be unable to survive, but also it can relate to whole communities. So in Madagascar child labour was necessary to survive in a harsh economic climate, but the children were not specifically exploited.*

3. *Unremunerated or hidden – this refers to work carried out within the family unit. While this is a feature of many developing economies it is also not uncommon in advanced nations.*

ACTIVITY **4.5**

Reconsider your response to the earlier question about work in the light of these categories. Consider both your own circumstances and that of families you may know. How far do these categories apply to children in the UK?

Comment

This may seem a more difficult question to answer, but it is likely that there are many children in the UK engaged in unremunerated work – a significant number being 'child carers' for example. Children who contribute to family businesses could see their labour as being part of a survival mechanism, but also potentially part of their 'career planning'. We are not condoning exploitative child labour here, but we do want you to think more widely about child labour in all its forms both in the UK and overseas. It is also worth remembering that child labour was a feature of Britain's own industrial development and many children did not receive a full secondary education until the implementation of the 1948 Education Act. The main distinction has to revolve around levels of exploitation, which increasingly is a consequence of globalisation and can be found in both the poor South and the rich North. The following extracts from a recent UNICEF campaign focusing upon the use of illegal child labour in the UK under the title of *Slave Britain* show how this is the case.

CASE STUDY

Natasha, a Romanian girl, was 12 years old when her mother died and her father turned to drink and abused her. She asked a friend to help and they fled across the border into Serbia and Montenegro. Her friend then sold her into prostitution, first in Albania, then in Italy, until finally she arrived in the UK. In the first six months she was prostituted and beaten by her trafficker. Supported by social workers, she helped bring her trafficker to justice and he was eventually sentenced to ten years' imprisonment.

Huy was a 15-year-old Vietnamese boy who was trafficked into the UK to work in a cannabis factory to pay off family debts. The factories are often in 'ordinary homes' but are dangerous places due to illegal electricity supplies and the chemicals used. The factory was raided and Huy was arrested. He was released on bail and referred to social services but went missing before he could be assessed.

(Source: UNICEF, 2007b, adapted)

Comment

The case studies demonstrate another side to the notion of 'economic well-being' for children who are trafficked, exploited and work illegally in a country where the labour of children is highly regulated. Childhood, global movement of labour and people trafficking (see Chapter 2) combine here, and often social workers are the people who are the ones who have to deal with the 'local' situations of children like Natasha and Huy.

Assessing in an international context

We have discussed at some length the exceptional situations that many refugee and asylum-seeking children find themselves in and how social workers are often at the forefront of interventions to improve the lives of these children. Much of social work in the UK is targeted at the first two ECM principles, that of being healthy and staying safe, in that work is often based upon the concept of 'risk'. If we consider the needs of children who are seeking asylum, we can also see that while they may be 'vulnerable', they are also 'resilient'. Nevertheless, they are also quite clearly 'children in need' and as such they would come into contact with social workers in the UK. Kohli (2006) very clearly outlines possible responses, and clearly draws upon other work which locates children firmly within their culture and tradition. This takes us to another area, where 'internationalisation' plays a distinct role: the concept of 'cultural diversity'.

Chapter 2 drew attention to the movement of labour, and demonstrated the extent of cultural diversity within the UK in discussions about the number of people born overseas and those who belonged to migrant groups. The earlier sections of this chapter, which deal with refugee children and those who have been exploited, highlight some of the more dramatic and shocking consequences of international forces. People move to other countries for different reasons, for example, to secure a better standard of living, often filling low-paid jobs in the receiving country. This was the case for some migrants to the UK from the Caribbean, Asia and Africa in the post-war years of the twentieth century. Here, we address what may be the more familiar ground of the experiences of Black and minority ethnic (BME) groups in the UK and the questions which social workers often face when assessing their needs.

RESEARCH SUMMARY

Chand (2001) undertook a systematic review of the literature in relation to the assessment of BME families, particularly in the area of child protection. This revealed that social workers were prone to accept certain stereotypes about the nature of Black families, as well as exhibiting a general trend to see such families as having 'weaknesses' rather than 'strengths'. Chand's research shows that misunderstandings continue to be a problem in the assessment of BME families. This raises issues concerning language difficulties and the use of interpreters, but more importantly about child-rearing practices, which vary from culture to culture. This research also draws attention to the poverty experienced by many BME groups and notes that there is a clear relationship between poverty and the incidences of child abuse, with poverty often leading to greater surveillance. Chand's research emphasises, however, that child abuse exists in all cultures and protection is a universal right.

Comment

One area which Chand touches on is the strength of other forms of child rearing and family. Carby (1982) wrote convincingly of the strength of the black family and argued that the family operated as both a haven from, and resistance to, the racism experienced by black people, including children. Families from other countries not only have different child-rearing practices, but they also experience other factors which make their position more vulnerable. With recent migrants we have explored how experiences prior to arriving in the UK may have been very traumatic, and that for many the trauma is not alleviated upon arrival. Other examples are provided throughout this book. It is also important to understand how aspects of the host society can impact upon people from other countries and cultures.

Identity and the importance of community and traditions

In Chapter 1, the idea of 'diaspora' was introduced. It is an important concept to understand in assessing families, since a way of maintaining a sense of personal and group identity is through holding on to cultural and religious practices. This can give a sense of belonging to people far from their homeland in another country, where the customs, religion and even climate are quite different. The first generation may hold on to their culture and religion, but attempt to assimilate into the host society. Jacoby (1999) explores the nature of migrant communities and argues that very often the second or third generation rejects the policies of integration followed by the parent first-generation migrants. This is a complex phenomenon which demonstrates the dynamic nature of culture. Jacoby (1999, p48) believes that ethnic pluralism derives from integrated communities who are *re-inventing the long lost roots of their grandparents: 'what the son wishes to forget, the grandson wishes to remember'*. The relevance for social workers dealing with second- or third-generation young people is that it is important to be aware that these young people might be searching for traditional expressions of culture and religion as a viable form of identity, which in part comes from the strong sense of their own community. This often happens when the community experiences disadvantage, as is the case with the Muslim communities in the UK (of Pakistani and Bangladeshi origin) and also the black African Caribbean communities. The young people from these ethnic groups have had the poorest educational attainment and job opportunities within the UK, something which also reflects the relatively low socio-economic status of these ethnic minority groups in general (Palmer, et al., 2005). The point we are making here is that general levels of social and economic deprivation are a feature of many migrant groups and these structural factors have to be taken into account by social workers who are engaged in assessing the needs of migrant children. (Price and Simpson, 2007).

RESEARCH SUMMARY

Graham (2002) sets out some points concerning issues relevant for assessment and intervention by social workers with children and families from other ethnic and cultural groups. She examines how African cultural practices have been seen as having a deficit, when they have been compared to Western approaches. She explores how African-centred cultures construct the family in a different way to the dominant UK and European view, which sees the nuclear family as the lens through which parenting and families are judged. Graham argues that these unfair and discriminatory views have resulted in an overrepresentation of black children in the public care system, the youth justice system and school exclusions. She sets out important areas for social workers to take into account in the African-centred world-view, as an aid to cultural sensitivity, as opposed to cultural relativism, which we discuss later in this chapter. For Graham these are:

RESEARCH SUMMARY

- *the interconnectedness of all things;*

- *the spiritual nature of human beings;*

- *collective/individual identity and the collective/inclusive nature of family structure;*

- *oneness of mind, body and spirit;*

- *the value of interpersonal relationships.*

Graham presents this in relation to African-centred world-views, but her attempts to understand the effect that culture has on how families are perceived is important in relation to how we construct our views, assessments and interventions for families from different ethnic and cultural traditions.

Comment

Graham raises important questions about the nature of culture and of child well-being. It is perhaps tempting to see the UK as a safe haven for children and to compare it positively with other countries. A UNICEF report on child well-being found that children in the UK regard themselves as less happy than other children in the advanced industrial nations. Other findings were that they were drinking more alcohol and taking more drugs and were more likely to experience failure at school along with violence and bullying. It is not surprising then that children generally had more unhappy and isolated relationships with both their families and peers, and young people rated their physical and mental health as poor – the worst of all among the rich nations of the world (Innocenti Research Centre, 2007).

Cultural identity

O'Hagan (1999, p273) argues that cultural identity is a sense of sameness and belonging and is the product of *values, ideas, perceptions and meaning, which have evolved over time*. For many migrant families their culture is a way of keeping connected to their past and Dosanjh and Ghuman (1997, p300) argue that *for many Punjabi families religion is the key element upon which their identity is nurtured and formed*. Such arguments may equally apply to Muslim and Hindu families. The recent arrival in the UK of significant numbers of Polish families, following the expansion of the EU, has seen a considerable increase in attendance at Roman Catholic churches. For many migrants, culture (often expressed through religion) has great significance for their personal identity. When it comes to aspects of child rearing, O'Hagan (1999, p27) suggests that bringing up children is largely determined by the culture into which a child is born and he cites Bretherton (1992) who argues that attachment theory is not merely 'instinctual' but the cultural context is significant for a child's emotional development.

Cultural relativism or sensitivity?

While it is important to understand the role that culture plays in understanding the nature of child rearing, it is vital for UK social workers to avoid engaging in a form of 'cultural relativism'. What this means is that social workers who have no knowledge of a particular culture (usually white, middle-class practitioners) ignore potentially abusive behaviour as being aspects of culture, which they should not criticise. By seeing different cultures in purely relative terms, false assumptions can be made about what is (and is not) acceptable and this can place children at even greater risk. Cultural sensitivity is needed, which understands the importance of culture in shaping identity, but which also allows social workers to protect children from abuse (Dingwall, et al., 1995).

We end with extracts from Lord Laming's report into the death of Victoria Climbié, which highlighted two cultural assumptions which were seemingly made. First, that respect and obedience were important features in the West African family, which explained Victoria having to stand to attention, *but* this was not a feature of life with her parents; and second, that children brought up in Africa may have more marks on their bodies than children raised in Europe. He commented that:

> *There is some evidence to suggest that one of the consequences of an exclusive focus on 'culture' in work with black children and families, is [that] it leaves black and ethnic minority children in potentially dangerous situations, because the assessment has failed to address a child's fundamental care and protection needs.*

(Laming, 2003, Part 5: 16.1)

Perhaps Lord Laming's most pertinent comment about the use or 'abuse' of culture is that:

> *There can be no excuse or justification for failing to take adequate steps to protect a vulnerable child, simply because that child's cultural background would make the necessary action somehow inappropriate.*

(16.11)

The important point to stress is that social workers need to be sensitive to culture and open to different patterns of child rearing but that this should *never* detract from protecting a child.

ACTIVITY 4.6

This activity will help you draw together the themes of the chapter in relation to cultural sensitivity. Read the chapter again, and note what you think would be the important aspects of being culturally sensitive in relation to some of the scenarios described.

Comment

There is much material to draw on and our comment is not an exhaustive 'check-list'. We anticipate that you have emphasised the idea of culture being evolved from values and shared experiences, so, when dealing with people who have a particular cultural expression, this needs to be a central part of the framework you use to understand their experiences. Graham's research summary is very useful in developing this understanding. The experience of migration will be part of this, and Kohli's work should alert you to many of the complexities in dealing with children and young people who have experienced traumatic life events, which is important when applied to the position of unaccompanied asylum-seeking children. We would also expect you to be aware of the points made at the end of this chapter, in reference to Dingwall, et al. (1995) and Lord Laming, about the need to ensure that sensitivity to culture does not lead to children being placed at risk.

C H A P T E R   S U M M A R Y

In this chapter we have set out key elements for UK-based social workers of how international perspectives impact upon their daily practice and have tried to build this around the *Every Child Matters* outcomes. So, after reading the chapter, you should have an appreciation of:

- definitions of childhood and how these differ from place to place and culture to culture in relation to needs;

- issues affecting refugee and asylum-seeking children in England and how the treatment of asylum-seeking children by the authorities, including social workers, measures up against social work's ethical codes;

- the experiences of children who are child soldiers in Africa, and child labourers in other countries, to demonstrate the different aspects of childhood globally;

- the situations faced by many children in England and other European countries as a result of child trafficking and exploitative labour;

- the challenges and complexities of assessing in an international context, exploring aspects of cultural identity and cultural sensitivity.

FURTHER READING

Beah, I (2007) *A long way gone: Memoirs of a boy soldier.* London: Fourth Estate.
Exactly as the title suggests, this book describes the memoirs of a child of 12 years old who became involved in the civil war in Sierra Leone.

Garrett, PM (2004) *Social work and Irish people in Britain: Historical and contemporary responses to Irish children and families.* Bristol: The Policy Press.
This book explores the relationship between social work and the Irish community in England and Wales for a group of people whose ethnicity has become increasingly invisible.

Graham, M (2007) *Black issues in social work and social care.* Bristol: The Policy Press.
This is a more recent text, which explores the experiences, values and world views of Black people and places them in the context of contemporary social work and social care practice.

Innocenti Research Centre (2007) *Report card 7: Child poverty in perspective: an overview of child well-being in rich countries – a comprehensive assessment of the lives and well-being of children and adolescents in the economically advanced nations.* Florence: United Nations Children's Fund (UNICEF).
This is the report referred to earlier, which you should read in full as it provides some insights into the nature of childhood and how it is experienced in the world's rich countries.

Chapter 5

International perspectives on social work with people with mental health issues

Janet E Williams, Jane Foggin and Marelize Joubert

A C H I E V I N G   A   S O C I A L   W O R K   D E G R E E

This chapter will help you to become familiar with the following National Occupational Standards for Social Work.

Key Role 6: Demonstrate professional competence in social work practice.

Unit 18 Research, analyse, evaluate, and use current knowledge of best social work practice.

Unit 20 Manage complex ethical issues, dilemmas and conflicts.

Unit 21 Contribute to the promotion of best social work practice.

It will also introduce you to the following academic standards set out in the Quality Assurance Agency social work subject benchmark statement.

4. Defining principles.

4.3 (...)

- Social work is located within different social welfare contexts. (...) In an international context, distinctive national approaches to social welfare policy, provision and practice have greatly influenced the focus and content of social work degree programmes.
- There are competing views in society at large on the nature of social work and on its place and purpose. Social work practice and education inevitably reflect these differing perspectives on the role of social work in relation to social justice, social care and social order.

5.1.1 Social work services, service users and carers.

- the social processes (associated with, for example, poverty, migration, unemployment, poor health, disablement, lack of education and other sources of disadvantage) that lead to marginalisation, isolation and exclusion, and their impact on the demand for social work services.

5.1.2 The service delivery context.

- the location of contemporary social work within historical, comparative and global perspectives, including European and international contexts;
- the issues and trends in modern public and social policy and their relationship to contemporary practice and service delivery in social work.

5.1.3 Values and ethics.

- the complex relationships between justice, care and control in social welfare and the practical and ethical implications of these, including roles as statutory agents and in upholding the law in respect of discrimination.

5.1.4 Social work theory.
- the relevance of sociological perspectives to understanding societal and structural influences on human behaviour at individual, group and community levels;
- user-led perspectives.

5.1.5 The nature of social work practice.
- the processes that facilitate and support service user choice and independence;
- the place of theoretical perspectives and evidence from international research in assessment and decision-making processes in social work practice.

Introduction

In this chapter, we will explore international perspectives on social work with people experiencing mental health difficulties. When working with any service user group, it is important for social workers to have an open mind for considering, and to be respectful of, a variety of perspectives (which can be competing with each other and with practitioners' own views). As previous chapters have already argued, international perspectives both require *and* help us to develop such an 'open mind'. Following this theme, in this chapter we will look at a variety of approaches to understanding, and responding to, people's experiences of mental ill health. This is a field of work where medicalised approaches, based on diagnoses, have since the late nineteenth century held a dominant position in countries of the global 'North'. We show that there are alternatives (which can compete with, enhance or complement this position) across different cultures (including within Europe and the UK), and we consider the importance of basing both social work practice and policy development on the experiences and involvement of service users.

Understanding mental health

What do we mean by 'mental (ill) health'?

ACTIVITY 5.1

Think about what is meant by mental health. How often do you differentiate between positive mental health and its more negative associations?

Comment

To begin the chapter we want to explore the idea of 'mental health' from a global perspective. As we have noted in the earlier chapters, it is easy to adopt an approach or understanding that is rooted in our own time and place, which often does not reflect global differences. When we consider 'mental health' we rarely consider what it means to have 'good mental health', since all too frequently the use of the term in countries of the 'global North' is connected with mental *ill* health. The World Health Organisation (WHO) defines mental health as

> *A state of well-being in which the individual realizes his or her ability, can cope with the normal stress of life, can work productively and fruitfully, and is able to make a contribution to his or her community.*

> (WHO, 2007a)

This definition describes a very positive and desirable state where individuals are 'in tune' with their society, and such a definition can be applied globally. It is also part of the notion of 'being healthy', as the WHO goes on to suggest that *health is a state of complete physical, mental and social well-being and not merely the absence of disease or infirmity* (*ibid*). Nevertheless, often just using the term 'mental health' is insufficient and it has become more common to use the terms 'positive mental health' or 'good mental health'.

On the other hand, we need to ask whether or not a definition of *poor* mental health, or mental *ill* health can simply be defined as the opposite of the earlier definition. When we begin to consider how mental ill health is defined, we move away from statements which are focused upon the relationship between people and society. Looking at definitions across a wide range of organisations (including WHO), we find that words such as 'symptoms', 'disorders' and 'diagnoses' are commonplace. They reflect what can be seen as the 'Northern' tradition, which emphasises a bio-medical model focusing upon an individual's (mal) functioning and pathology. Pilgrim and Rogers (1999, p23) argue that this tradition has ignored *the normal in favour of the abnormal.* One in four people develop mental ill health at some point; moreover there are also very strong links between mental ill health and structural factors, especially poverty (WHO, 2007b).

Global perspectives

The medicalised definition, and the reliance on diagnoses, also sometimes referred to as the *Northern bio-medical model* of mental health is contested by some groups of service users and mental health practitioners because it ignores social, economic and environmental causation and implies that mental health problems are not a *normal* part of most people's lives (Pilgrim and Rogers, 1999). Those who challenge it also point out that a psychiatric diagnosis is not based on scientifically proved causations, which is the basis of diagnosis in physical medicine, and they therefore question the validity of the core tool of psychiatry – the diagnosis.

Bio-medical understandings of mental ill health are not universal. Read the following brief summary of research which sought to examine different understandings of mental ill health.

> **RESEARCH SUMMARY**
>
> ### *Dr Alta van Dyk – Western and African responses to mental health*
>
> *In a study of 137 Black Zulu-speaking and 142 white English-speaking South Africans, van Dyk (2001) identified different understandings of mental health. For the Zulu-speaking Africans this was related to* collective responsibility, co-operation with others, and harmony with their neighbours and ancestors. *The white, English-speaking Africans had entirely different associations for 'good' mental health, which were* individuality,

independence, and self-sufficiency. *Not surprisingly, these two contrasting understandings of good mental health resulted in quite different approaches to mental ill health. The Black Africans dealt with episodes of stress through communal activities of singing, danc-*ing, and mutual discussion *– i.e. they sought to reconnect to the community through group activity. The white Africans in the study, on the other hand, were more likely to choose* therapy, medication, and relaxation techniques.

(Adapted from the British Psychological Society, 2009)

Comment

Van Dyk highlights the contrasting understandings of people of different ethnic backgrounds in the same country. Such an approach is valuable in raising questions about how 'Northern' explanations and understandings of mental ill health dominate. This is part of a theme in her overall research, which focuses on the unsuitability of 'Northern' or 'Western' AIDS treatment programmes in Africa.

The significance of van Dyk's research extends beyond South Africa, indicating that there are likely to be clear cultural differences in understanding and responding to mental ill health. Maiello (2008), a Western-trained psychotherapist, discusses her meeting with a traditional African healer. She argues that there are differences and similarities in the approaches, but that both approaches are rooted in their own cultural traditions. Crucially the role of ancestors as revered *internal objects* in African cultures is identified, as well as the need for a culturally sensitive understanding. Differing approaches to mental wellbeing can also be found within cultures of south-east Asia, where people are seen as a *physical, emotional, mental and spiritual being* (Mental Health Foundation, 2004). In other words, bio-medical categorisations of mental health and/or physical health, and the separation of emotion and spirituality from well-being are not present in these cultures.

Different world-views: spirituality and emotion

There is an uneasy relationship between religion, spirituality and psychological and psychiatric explanation of mental distress (Barker and Buchanan-Barker, 2005). The hearing of voices and interceding with ancestors do not fit with the scientific rationalism of psychiatry, yet they play a large part in many people's lives. We have to set aside our own explanations, our own world-view to some extent, if we genuinely seek to connect with people who have different world-views and wish to help them understand their experience of mental distress.

If we are outside communities who use traditional healers it is not possible to fully understand their significance; but the identified benefits of traditional healers are recognisable.

- *People are helped to make sense of their symptoms. Traditional healers use traditional and culturally relevant explanations, based on a full understanding of the individual as an integral component of a family and a community. In this role they have a high status and are looked up to. This is because they are an integral part of the community and they are expected to use their powers to benefit the good of the people.*

- *Taking a holistic approach, traditional healers give people time to fully express their fears, thus demonstrating that they take the person and their symptoms seriously.*

- *Members of the family participate fully in the treatment process.* (Kale, 1995, pp1182-5)

Social models and service users

Even in countries of the global 'North', where the bio-medical model is considered dominant, there are alternative ways of understanding mental ill health. There is a significant set of social understandings of mental ill health, which seek to locate it within the range of social circumstances people find themselves in (Tew and Foster, 2005, p3). This sometimes connects with *issues of powerlessness and loss.* There is a significant body of work which addresses the importance of 'the social' in understanding mental ill health, for example the social constructionism of Szasz (1971), the anti-psychiatry movement of Cooper (1968) and Laing (1967) and the so-called Frankfurt school which attempted to synthesise the work of Freud and Marx (see, for example Fromm, 2002). With equal significance, the work of Foucault (1967; 1977) is important because this stood outside of the 'mental health tradition' and developed the concept that the interventions for people experiencing mental ill health, notably psychiatry, were primarily concerned with aspects of surveillance and social control, rather than care and compassion. This very brief summary shows that there has been a long-standing tradition opposed to bio-medical models within the 'Northern' tradition. The social models also form the basis of the more recent service user movements (Hopton, 2006) to which we now turn.

One way of understanding mental ill health is through the experiences of those who have lived through it. Many of these people are deeply critical of the type of services provided and also of how such services create and sustain negative stereotypes of 'mentally ill' people, themes which we will explore later in the chapter. Frequently the areas of conflict are around 'diagnosis' and 'treatment'. In an account of service user perspectives, Cree and Davis (2006, p64) report the words of a Northern Irish service user, Maggie, who experienced a false diagnosis: *I knew this was wrong. But at the time, I didn't know how to fight to get anything changed on that. It took me a long while to convince people.* She went on to say that what mattered was not the (bio-medical) diagnosis but how the condition affects people. For many, the most effective form of treatment is not from professionals, but through self-help groups. As another service user, Trish, explains:

> *What I love about the day centre is the ethos of the place, where people are encouraged to take on responsibility for themselves, for the centre, and to work towards trying to change mental health services from the inside.*
>
> (Cree and Davis, 2006, p72)

Who experiences mental ill health?

The previous section sought to outline different approaches to understanding mental well-being and ill health, and concluded with accounts from service users. We will now explore these experiences in more detail and examine some of the more prevalent factors which cause mental ill health. The WHO (2001) suggests that mental ill health affects around one in four people globally. That is why, when trying to answer the question 'Whom does it affect?', the response is that *life events, stress and the strength of our support networks, together with our age or gender, all combine in determining our mental health; that is why anyone can potentially develop a mental health problem* (Rethink, 2007).

The causes of mental ill health can be varied – some argue that they are internal (based, for example, on biological factors), while others stress the influence of the social or external environment, such as exposure to stressful events. For many people it could be a combination of the two, in that the same event could result in a different response. This section will now focus upon causes and experiences of mental ill health using a global perspective, highlighting that many factors are the same, wherever people live.

Trauma and disasters

In many parts of the world, natural disasters are as frequent as they are devastating. The tsunami of 2004 was one of the most devastating disasters of recent times. In the aftermath, the WHO was active in developing provision in the six countries directly affected by it.

ACTIVITY 5.2

Read the summary below and think about the issues raised and how they could be addressed within that particular culture.

Naaz's story: Battling the demons of the mind
That fateful day felt just like any other as she got ready for work. Naaz was all alone in the house, when the tsunami struck. She was taking a leisurely shower, when she heard a muffled roar. She ventured outside to find water gushing into the room. Within minutes the water level rose at an alarming rate. Naaz kicked and struggled to stay afloat as the room filled up with water. The door gave way and Naaz was dragged down the road by a tempestuous surge of water. Just when it looked as though she would be swept out to sea, she reached out and grabbed the nearest solid structure she could lay her hands on. Her struggle for survival against the relentless onslaught of water was over for the time being, but it was an image that would play over and over again in her mind for a long time.

(WHO, 2005, p25)

Comment

This excerpt is from the WHO report about the reconstruction of the Maldives after the tsunami. It goes on to describe how Naaz is still 'tormented' by those events, that she had recurring nightmares, anxiety attacks, and that it took her a long time to return to the island of Muli, where these events happened. Conway, et al. (2002, p235) had written about the problems involved in transferring one set of solutions, located within a 'Northern' culture (in this instance Australia) to 'Southern' situations, and they concluded that *cultural and contextual circumstances necessitate a critical appraisal of the needs of the community and the corresponding attributes of those who provide healthcare services. This means designing programmes that are ... easily adapted to different circumstances.* Many of the communities affected were in countries where there was a lack of mental health services and also a degree of stigma attached to mental ill health, though 'diagnoses' of post-traumatic stress disorder are much more acceptable, since these are viewed as outcomes of unforeseen events (Kokai, et al., 2004). Anderson (2007), describing her work in Indonesia after the tsunami, provides a clue to how people like Naaz accessed the support they required to begin to readjust to their world after the disaster. People's main concern was with their families and livelihoods and it was in this context that questions about the psychological effects of the tsunami could be approached. More significant was the means of delivering support, which was through the establishment of community-based groups and programmes which attempted to teach 'self-help' support, drawing upon established community traditions and culture.

ACTIVITY 5.3

In many parts of the world, people are affected by war, as well as other disasters. The negative impact this will have upon mental health is clear. In earlier chapters the position of asylum seekers has been discussed, especially the traumatising effects of being a child soldier (see Chapter 4). Read through these sections again, and reconsider them in the light of this chapter about mental health. A particularly useful section to revisit will be the research summary of Kohli's (2006) work.

RESEARCH SUMMARY

Here are summaries of two pieces of research which sought to explore responses to terrorist attacks in Kenya (Nairobi) and the USA (Oklahoma).

Njenga, et al. (2004)
Njenga, et al. (2004) argue that most studies of post-traumatic stress disorder (PTSD) following terrorist attacks have been conducted in Northern (industrialised) countries, have been based upon small samples and have been undertaken several months or even years after the incident. The US embassy in Nairobi was bombed in 1998 and the researchers aimed to study a Southern ('non-Western') group of people soon after the attack and examine their responses. Over 2,800 Kenyans answered a self-report questionnaire within three months of the attack. The authors found that in 35 per cent of responses there was evidence of PTSD. Key factors were gender (more women than men were affected); whether or not people saw the blast and/or were injured by it; bereavement (as a consequence of the attack); not speaking to a friend about the attack; people's educational background; and financial difficulties as a consequence of the blast. The important conclusion was that specific factors, which are thought to predict short-term responses to post-traumatic stress were confirmed in this large and 'non-Western' sample.

North, et al. (2005)
The aim in this study was to compare responses of Kenyans who witnessed the Nairobi bombings with Americans who witnessed the Oklahoma bombings. The important findings were that rates of PTSD and major depression after the bombings were similar. The main differences were that the Nairobi group relied more on religious support and the Oklahoma City group used more medical treatment, drugs, and alcohol. It is the differences in responding to the bombings which are of significance here. There were strong similarities between the two cultures in how people were affected, but coping responses and treatment were quite different.

Comment

The significance of these findings lies in their combined conclusions. Responses which may trigger mental ill health are similar across cultures, but how these are dealt with differs between cultures. One issue, however, which is raised in both pieces, is that financial difficulties (or relative poverty) could be both a consequence of the traumatic event and also a cause of stress. This means that those who, in relative terms, were poorer, were more adversely affected. This leads us into the discussion of another factor, which has a global significance: poverty.

Poverty

The relationship between poverty and mental ill health is well established. If people are poor, they are more likely to experience mental ill health than those who are relatively wealthy. Globally, many of the instances we have already discussed in this section feature the experiences of people who are already poor, and whose lives have been made even more impoverished by the effects of war and/or natural disasters.

RESEARCH SUMMARY

Fryer and labour market disadvantage (1995)

The links between unemployment and mental ill health are long-standing. Fryer (1995) identifies three important factors which occur when someone loses their job. First, there is the obvious reduction in income and financial impoverishment. Second, for many there is the loss of social status. Third, Fryer identifies the reduction in 'agency', which he describes as losing a sense of purpose and self-esteem, which are associated with earning a wage. He also notes that the impact is not confined to the person who has lost their job, but also affects their families. This would include children, whose school performance may suffer. The possible consequences include: an increased risk of depression; alcohol dependency; anxiety states; and psychosomatic reactions. Fryer suggests that these outcomes could also be seen in those who were either in low-paid work or insecure jobs. He points out that the very real material impact of poverty on its own, combined with the resulting social exclusion can lead to increasing mental ill health.

ACTIVITY **5.4**

In the light of this research summary, consider how a deep worldwide recession, following the events of September 2008, will impact upon people in 'Northern' and 'Southern' countries in terms of mental well-being.

Comment

A recession results in increased rates of unemployment and so, following the work of Fryer, we could expect to see increased numbers of people experiencing mental ill health. We could also expect to see the consequences adversely affecting their families. We could speculate that if whole communities are affected by job losses, then these negative effects could impair the provision of community-based support. An alternative view is that if everyone is affected, then a sense of community solidarity could have a positive effect. However, while becoming unemployed can have a significant negative impact upon mental well-being, mental ill health can also come from employment. A major cause of this is workplace stress (Bunting, 2005), and this is increasing among all socio-economic groups. Faragher, et al. (2005) found that workplace stress was largely linked to a reduction in job satisfaction. Automated work processes reduce the control workers have over their work, and while this is measured in Northern countries, we should also remember that in more recent years global capitalism has shifted many routine jobs from the North to the developing South (see Chapter 2). This change in work patterns is likely to have similar consequences for these workers.

Stress and sudden life changes

Everyone experiences life changes and common life changes include: the death of a partner, relative or close friend; serious illness; losing a job; getting a new job; marriage; divorce; and moving house. For many people, especially in Northern countries, the traumas of war and natural disasters are seen on our television screens. As with poverty, there are a number of experiences which can induce episodes of mental ill health across all cultures.

ACTIVITY 5.5

For an example of how different factors combine, read the following extract from Cree and Davis (2006, p64) which describes Helen's experience.

My husband had been under a lot of pressure through his job … Living in Northern Ireland there were added pressures from the situation and from his role as a manager of a social club. He had had experience at the hands of paramilitaries … for about two years before he became ill, I knew there was something … and something was going to give. I always thought it would be … a heart attack or a stroke. I never … imagined it would be mental health problems.

Here we can see workplace pressures and those of a society in conflict and crisis combining, and affecting individuals and families. The WHO definition of positive mental health should be recalled, since this (and the other examples in this section) are situations where people are not in a state of well-being in which the individual realises his or her abilities, can cope with the normal stresses of life, can work productively and fruitfully, and is able to make a contribution to his or her community.

You will have noticed that one of the sudden life changes which generate a level of stress is moving house. One of the themes of this book concerns 'journeys'; not just those involved when people move house, but also those of moving from one community or country and settling somewhere else: internal and international migration demonstrate the notion that 'the global is local'. We now turn to examine the experiences of black and minority ethnic (BME) groups in the UK, a situation where indeed the global has become local.

The global is local: Mental ill health experiences of Black and minority ethnic groups

To gain an understanding of how BME groups experience mental ill health, read the following stories, which were introduced in Chapter 1.

ACTIVITY 5.6

As you read the following accounts of two people with very different backgrounds, consider how their histories and experiences may have contributed to their current mental ill health.

Portia's story

Portia came to the UK in 1960 from the Caribbean and brought up a family here. She has had contact with the mental health services for herself and as a carer for her youngest son Raymond who has been diagnosed as having schizophrenia.

Portia found work, albeit low paid and lacking status. She worked hard all her life, married and brought up her children. Thus Portia's position was different from Ali's because she was an economic migrant who, because she was helped to migrate by the UK Government, had nothing to prove to immigration authorities and was not fleeing intolerable conditions and traumatic events. However, she experienced fear, racism, poverty and lack of acceptance from the local community just like other Black and minority ethnic (BME) groups and asylum seekers.

Portia had always planned to return to her home country. In Chapter 6, we see Warnes and Williams's (2006) typology, which describes Portia as someone who has aged in place (see Chapter 6 for a full discussion of this). She might have explored the possibility of returning home using the International Social Services UK (ISS UK) if she were not the main carer for her son Raymond. Her depression is linked to her wish to return home and the realisation that she no longer has meaningful links there.

Ali's story

Ali fled from torture in Iraq hoping to find safety in the UK. We do not know much about Ali's childhood or whether he had any mental health problems before he was tortured. We do know that being tortured means that he, and probably his family, will have experienced threats, physical and psychological abuse and terror. His family was killed in Iraq and the social networks he grew up with either turned against him or were unable to protect him because he was targeted for torture.

There are two parts to his story and those of other asylum seekers in relation to mental health: firstly, the impact of the experiences in the home country and the journey to escape; and, secondly, the life experienced on arrival as an asylum seeker in the UK. Once Ali had his request for asylum accepted he was termed a refugee. The United Nations High Commissioner for Refugees (UNHCR) has a legal definition for refugees as people who are outside their countries because of a well-founded fear of persecution based on their race, religion, nationality, political opinion or social group (United Nations Convention and Protocol relating to the Status of Refugees, 1951, Article 1 A (2)).

Comment

Portia's depression could be linked to the stress of being a Black carer for her son Raymond. There are a number of structural differences between BME group carers' needs and those of other carers in the mental health field. This means that they are more likely to experience poor health, social exclusion and live in poverty, and are less likely to be claiming benefits. Complex cultural dynamics, for example the need to remain in line with the community's expectations, may mean that carers are isolated from others caring for people experiencing mental health difficulties; alternatively they could 'come out of the cultural box' and be seen to be rejecting the community norms. This could result in a severe loss of cultural support. There may be tensions between the service's expectations about disability and independence in relation to mental health and those of the community. There may be questions of family honour or shame if there is a full recognition, through attendance at mental health services, of mental illness within the family. The services too may make assumptions that the community may want to look after its own rather than checking whether specialist or mainstream services are the preferred option (Carers UK, 2007).

There has been little research into the mental health experiences of African-Caribbean women. Race equality initiatives concentrate mostly on Black men, and gender initiatives mostly benefit white women (the Parekh Report, 2000), so Portia's mental health needs, as a Black African-Caribbean woman, are generally marginalised within an already marginalised group (Mind, 2006).

When thinking about Ali, you need to understand something about the experiences that lead people to leave their homes and culture. The experience of war and violence is common among many refugees and asylum seekers. Consequences of these experiences include: people's sense of self being destroyed because of persistent states of fear and vulnerability; the destroying of people's status within their community, for example as a result of rape. People may have lived in areas where family and neighbours are expected to report on each other, which destroys trust and mutual support. Homes and property may have been destroyed; food removed; massacres could have taken place; children may have been kidnapped to become soldiers; or in the case of girls to be taken as sexual slaves for the army. Gender abuse, through systematic rape, is often used against civilians of all ages, particularly women, and including children, while others may be made to witness it.

Sometimes, institutions for people who are 'mentally ill' are the locations for carrying out ill treatment and torture (see Office for the United Nations High Commission for Human Rights, 2006). When we think about the experiences of war and the resulting need to escape in the context of the definitions of mental well-being and mental ill health, it is not difficult to see how such experiences may lead to mental ill health.

While these two case studies are very different, they tell us much about the experience of people who have moved from one cultural sphere to another, and they bring home one of the central themes of the book, that the local is global. The local experiences of BME groups in the UK are often a consequence of the local and global combining.

You may also have thought about Raymond, Portia's son. Young men from BME communities are particularly vulnerable to mental ill health because they are subject to discrimination and social exclusion. Raymond is also likely to be discriminated against when he tries to access or receive mental health services.

Commission for Health Care Audit and Inspection (2005) Count Me In

The Health Care Commission's (2005) Count Me In census of inpatients in mental health hospitals and facilities in England and Wales found that disproportionately high numbers of young African-Caribbean males are in the UK's mental health system, and their experiences are often harsh, with high levels of detention, seclusion, restraint and assault (Walls and Sashidharan 2003). For example, Black men are more likely to experience doses over the recommended limit of powerful medication, and physical restraints in hospitals, prisons and police stations. In comparison to white men, 'talking therapies' and recovery approaches are less likely to be offered. In addition, lengths of stay in hospital are also significantly higher than average for many minority groups. The Mental Health Act Commission (2008) found that the UK's mental health services focus primarily on medication, maintenance and control while opportunities for recovery are limited. Statistical data showed that Black African-Caribbean people are:

- *10 per cent of mental health inpatients but only 3 per cent of the general population (2001 census);*

- *50 per cent more likely to be placed in seclusion;*

- *29 per cent more likely to be subject to control and restraint;*

- *44 per cent more likely to be sectioned under the 1983 Mental Health Act;*

- *50 per cent more likely to be referred through the criminal justice system;*

- *14 per cent more likely to be turned away than white people when they ask for help from mental health services.*

In addition,

- *referral to psychiatric services by the police is almost double for Black Caribbeans and Black Africans;*

- *referral through the courts is almost double for Black African and Caribbean people.*

In many ways the data speaks for itself. It leads to a view of the UK's mental health system as being 'institutionally racist', which Macpherson (1999, para. 6.34) defined as:

> *[The] collective failure of an organisation to provide an appropriate and professional service to people because of their colour, culture or ethnic origin. It can be seen or detected in processes, attitudes and behaviour which amount to discrimination through unwitting prejudice, ignorance, thoughtlessness and racist stereotyping, which disadvantage minority ethnic people.*

We can see that in the case of the UK, people who have journeyed here from overseas (or whose ancestors have done so) can experience a range of discrimination in relation to the services they receive. This leads us to consider the final part of this chapter, which is national and local policy for people who experience mental ill health.

'Mental health' policy

This concluding section will examine aspects of policies for people who experience mental ill health, drawing together strands from earlier discussions. Mental health policy is a viable field of study in its own right, and the following short section can hardly do justice to it. What we want to try to do here is focus upon key policy aspects within the Northern tradition, with examples from the UK, Ireland, the USA and Italy. You should refer back to other sections to see how other understandings of mental ill health could potentially lead to different policy outcomes.

One of the factors we have stressed here is the universality of experiencing mental ill health so that we can avoid the notion of 'them and us'. We have already discussed how poverty and structural disadvantage lead to higher rates of mental ill health. We can add to this the experience of racism for people who belong to established BME groups as well as those seeking asylum in the UK (and, for that matter, 'Northern' countries in general). A feature which links all people who experience mental ill health is stigma. Stigma associated with mental distress is an aggravating factor because it brings shame and fear, although this varies between communities. Shame and stigma affect the likelihood of families seeking help and diminish the chance of survivors regaining their self-esteem (Seebohm 2008). An example is this account given by Sally, a woman from Northern Ireland:

> *I have felt like a freak – you know, the name calling – from neighbours – folk who are just ignorant of mental illness. We are now trying to break down some of the stigma, because people don't really understand – they are scared. Mental illness is so different to a physical illness ... with certain types of depression you cannot see it; no one can see it.*

> (Cree and Davis, 2006, p65)

Another contributor goes further and comments that the distrust is not just confined to neighbours and acquaintances, but within the sufferer's own family, and she concludes that *if our own families do that, what chance do we have in the rest of the population?* (Cree and Davis, 2006, p65). The WHO (2008a) has identified the reduction of stigma as being a key target for promoting positive mental health.

It could be argued that successive policies, especially, but not only, in the UK and Northern countries, have helped create and sustain attitudes of 'them and us', thereby adding to the stigma people experience. It was commonplace for people experiencing mental ill health to be separated from the rest of the community in asylums or specialist hospitals, especially in the developed North. This type of provision is important in understanding policy, but it is also important to note that there have always been opponents to it, going back to the nineteenth century (Scull, 1983). For Scull, and many others, policy towards people who experience mental ill health is located within a politics of social control and of maintaining a certain 'social order'. While all policies in social welfare have elements of social control, in this arena it is more marked, and the epitome of it is the asylum, famously analysed by Goffman (1961).

Movements away from the asylum towards community approaches began in the USA in the 1960s but gathered pace in the 1970s (Scull, 1977). In the UK the 'decarceration process' gathered pace in the 1980s. Community approaches dominate contemporary policy.

The position is not alike in all European countries. A well-known example of an alternative approach to policy is the experience of Italy. This is summarised below, drawing upon the work of Donnelly (1992) and the experience of an academic exchange in an area of northern Italy (Trieste) by one of the authors of this chapter (Janet Williams).

POLICY SUMMARY

Closing the asylum – the Italian experience

Led by an Italian psychiatrist, Franco Basaglia, the Psichiatria Democratica (Democratic Psychiatry) undertook a sustained campaign to change Italy's policy, by drawing attention to the plight of people in asylums and specialist institutions. It culminated in 1978, when the Italian Government passed Law 180 which required:

- *the closure of all the existing single-purpose asylums, including no further new admissions nor any readmissions to them;*

- *new Community Mental Health Centres to be established;*

- *wards in general hospitals could be used.*

All new centres should:

- *include all services including emergency day and night services;*

- *act as the focus for mental health services in a locality, with some support from general hospitals;*

- *should be staffed by multidisciplinary teams with nurses, social workers, sociologists and latterly psychologists, led by a psychiatrist.*

The criteria for admission were quite radical since they separated the needs of the individual for treatment from society's concern with social control and antisocial behaviour. The former is the realm of the mental health system while the latter is that of the criminal justice system which has its own medical and psychiatric services.

The changes to the services were based upon five key concepts.

1. Deinstitutionalisation at the patient's pace.

2. Being with the patient, spending time and understanding.

3. Integration – of all emarginati ('marginalised people') into the community and inviting the community to participate in activities of the mental health services.

4. Social, anti-psychotherapeutic approach emphasising work and living conditions.

5. Involvement in local politics, psychiatrists establishing the needs of mentally ill within the town.

Not all areas in Italy adopted Law 180. However, it remains an example of how a process of deinstitutionalisation can proceed, and was underpinned by a different understanding of mental ill health from a prevailing one based upon a bio-medical model. These changes have not been without their critics who point to the resulting chaos which ensued. The point is to argue here that policy can have different formulations, and different traditions (and here it is the 'anti-psychiatry tradition' which we referred to earlier).

In some Northern countries similar processes have been much more rapid with less concern showed for the individual, and have led to new forms of community-based social control (Scull, 1977), aspects of which can be seen in Portia and Raymond's story.

Service users and 'recovery'

The service user movement has had an impact upon policy in recent years. Recovery as an approach involves personal development and change, including an acceptance that there are problems to face, a sense of involvement and control over one's life, the cultivation of hope and using the support of others, including direct collaboration in joint problem-solving between people using services, workers and professionals. Recovery starts with the individual and works from the inside out (Rethink, 2004). The recovery approach has it origins within service user groups in the USA (National Alliance on Mental Illness Santa Cruz County, 2005) and is often associated with Pat Deegan (1996), an American psychologist and service user. The Irish Government Special Report, *A Vision for Change,* argued that services should be developed and organised around the concept.

> *A recovery approach should inform every level of the service provision so service users learn to understand and cope with their mental health difficulties, build on their inherent strengths and resourcefulness, establish supportive networks, and pursue dreams and goals that are important to them and to which they are entitled as citizens.*
>
> (Government of Ireland, 2006, p7)

To promote recovery practitioners in the mental health arena need to:

- understand that recovery is a process unique to each person;
- understand the role of hope in the recovery process;
- accept that recovery is not about the elimination of symptoms or the notion of a 'cure';
- work in a way that is flexible and responds to the expressed needs of the person.

(Department of Health, 2004a, p19)

The principles of recovery can be seen to be based upon the principles of positive mental health and how to achieve this state. It can be argued that recovery stands within one of the Northern traditions, but it also has much in common with other traditions, which are focused upon a holistic notion of well-being. The use of recovery shows a policy shift away from the institutional approach, which sought to control people through segregation and to reinforce aspects of 'normality' through the 'incarceration' of the deviant (Cohen and Scull, 1983). The approach has come from service users and is being incorporated into mainstream services. In this way it is an example of how policy can be shaped and influenced not only from above, but also 'from below' by those who use services and experience mental ill health.

CHAPTER SUMMARY

In this chapter, we have considered different approaches to understanding and defining 'mental health' and 'mental ill health' in an international context. We have also looked at various factors which influence people's experiences of mental ill health from the perspective that 'the global is local is global' (see Chapter 2). In summary, we think that the following points are important.

- While in countries of the global 'North', the bio-medical model of understanding mental ill health (relying on psychiatric diagnosis and medical treatment) has been dominant, alternative approaches exist both in the global 'South' and within the traditions of 'Northern' countries. From an international perspective, a medicalised approach to mental ill health not only contrasts with traditional healing models focusing on spirituality, but has also met with long-standing opposition from proponents of social models and from service users.

- Looking at people's experiences of mental ill health, an international perspective highlights that responses to exceptional life events, such as disaster and trauma, are similar across different cultures, but people deal with the aftermath of such events and the 'symptoms' they experience in different ways. Services offering help need to take account of these issues.

- Poverty, work-related stress and sudden life changes are also important factors for considering the causes of mental ill health. From an international perspective, migration is a particularly significant life-changing experience. In the case of refugees and asylum seekers, people's reasons for moving from one country to another can themselves be associated with trauma, and social workers must have an understanding of these issues. On the other hand, being a member of a black and minority ethnic group increases, for many service users in the UK, the likelihood of experiencing discrimination and institutionalised racism from the very services that should be offering them help and support.

- From an international perspective, there are varying approaches to 'mental health' policies – but a challenge for all of them is how to deal with the stigma still attached to mental ill health. In many countries, there has been a movement away from 'institutionalising' people suffering mental ill health, towards providing community-based services. Whether such services merely substitute one form of 'social control' with another, or whether they are led by service users' needs and perspectives, seems to depend on the extent to which 'recovery' is appreciated as a holistic concept based on the strengths, resourcefulness, flexibility and hopes inherent in individuals and their communities.

FURTHER READING

Beresford, P (2006) *Human rights: Transforming services.*
www.scie.org.uk/news/events/humanrights06/PeterBeresford.pdf
A service user perspective on human rights, mental health and service user involvement.

Kesey, K (1962) *One flew over the cuckoo's nest.* (Originally published in 1962, but reprinted in numerous editions – e.g. Penguin Classics.)
A classic novel set in a mental institution in 1950s America. The book has also been turned into an Academy Award-winning film (1975), directed by Milos Forman and starring Jack Nicholson.

Salinger, JD (1994: first published 1951) *The catcher in the rye.* London: Penguin.
A controversial classic story about a young man's breakdown.

Chapter 6

International aspects of social work with elders

Sue Lawrence and Graeme Simpson

This chapter will enable you to become familiar with the following National Occupational Standards for Social Work.

Key Role 1: Prepare for, and work with individuals, families, carers, groups and communities to assess their needs and circumstances.

Unit 1 Prepare for social work contact and involvement.

1.3 Evaluate all information to identify the best form of initial involvement.

Key Role 6: Demonstrate professional competence in social work practice.

Unit 18 Research, analyse, evaluate, and use current knowledge of best social work practice.

19.3 Work within the principles and values underpinning social work practice.

Unit 20 Manage complex ethical issues, dilemmas and conflicts.

It will also introduce you to the following academic standards set out in the social work subject benchmark statement.

5.1.1 Social work services, service users and carers.
- the social processes (associated with, for example, poverty, migration, unemployment, poor health, disablement, lack of education and other sources of disadvantage) that lead to marginalisation, isolation and exclusion, and their impact on the demand for social work services;
- explanations of the links between definitional processes contributing to social differences (for example, social class, gender, ethnic differences, age, sexuality and religious belief) and the problems of inequality and differential need faced by service users;
- the nature of social work services in a diverse society (with particular reference to concepts such as prejudice, interpersonal, institutional and structural discrimination, empowerment and anti-discriminatory practices);
- the nature and validity of different definitions of, and explanations for, the characteristics and circumstances of service users and the services required by them, drawing on knowledge from research, practice experience, and from service users and carers;
- the focus on outcomes, such as promoting the well-being of young people and their families, and promoting dignity, choice and independence for adults receiving services.

5.1.2 The service delivery context.
- the location of contemporary social work within historical, comparative and global perspectives, including European and international contexts.

5.1.3 Values and ethics.
- aspects of philosophical ethics relevant to the understanding and resolution of value dilemmas and conflicts in both interpersonal and professional contexts.

5.1.4 Social work theory.
- the relevance of sociological perspectives to understanding societal and structural influences on human behaviour at individual, group and community levels;
- the relevance of psychological, physical and physiological perspectives to understanding personal and social development and functioning;
- user-led perspectives.

5.1.5 The nature of social work practice.
- the processes that facilitate and support service user choice and independence;
- the place of theoretical perspectives and evidence from international research in assessment and decision-making processes in social work practice;
- the integration of theoretical perspectives and evidence from international research into the design and implementation of effective social work intervention, with a wide range of service users, carers and others.

Introduction

International social work has been described as a *lens through which to view local social work* (Lyons, et al., 2006, p11) and in this chapter we will explore how taking an international perspective can help bring important insights into social work with elders. In order to do this, we need to explore some of the international elements contained within the field of social work with elders, which include:

- knowledge of the different contexts for social work with elders and social welfare in and beyond the UK;

- skills in working with elders from and between different countries, cultures and minority groups;

- values which respect difference and promote the principles of human rights and social justice for elders.

We will utilise information from international statistics, and from policies and practice in a variety of countries to seek international perspectives to the points raised above. We hope that using this international lens will help you to view local social work with elders in a more critical and reflective way.

What is the context for social work with elders?

Let us begin by considering how we understand the term *elders* and explore some of the factors that might influence that understanding. It is difficult to be precise about when we would call someone *old* as people age very differently according to factors such as lifestyle and health. The culture and norms of the society in which we live help to inform our view of what is considered to be *old age*. Our perception of age also changes according to our own age. As we grow older ourselves, our understanding of old age changes and becomes linked, among other things, to the length of time we would expect someone to live.

Different terms are used to describe elders, for example, older people, senior citizens, seniors. We have chosen to use the term 'elders' as this denotes respect and wisdom and is in common usage in many communities and nations.

Ageing populations

Most populations in the world are described as *ageing*, or *greying*, which means that the proportion of elders in the general population is getting larger (George, 1997). One reason for this is a declining number of births in many countries resulting in fewer young people aged below 16 years in the general population. At the same time, improved diet, public health, living conditions and advances in health care have resulted in a general rise in life expectancy in many countries and has contributed to an increase in the population of the number of people aged over 65 years (Phillips, et al., 2006, p9).

Country-based age differences

In the UK the average life expectancy from birth is 77 years for men and 81 years for women (World Health Organisation, 2008b). In sub-Saharan Africa, however, many people live on average only until their early forties (CIA World Factbook, 2009). In Africa, internal wars and conflicts, the HIV/AIDS pandemic, drought and malnutrition have claimed many young lives. In Russia, the average life expectancy in 2006 was 65 years (UNICEF, 2009) with male life expectancy recently declining to 59 years. In countries such as these, old age is obviously viewed differently and tends to be thought of as being relatively earlier than in countries with a higher life expectancy. In all developed countries older women out-number older men, as women tend to live longer (Arber, 2006, p62).

Different experiences of old age based on ethnicity

The population of elders is becoming increasingly diverse due to globalising processes. An international perspective on social work with elders requires us to understand the context for that diversity if we are to practise knowledgeably and sensitively across and between the many cultures and ethnicities in elder populations in the UK.

RESEARCH SUMMARY

In the UK 2001 population census, 4 per cent of the population described themselves as 'black'. Of those people, 15 per cent were 50 years and above (around 672,000 people), whereas in the total population, 33 per cent were 50 and over. Of the black population, people from the Caribbean had the largest proportion of their population aged 65 and over at 11 per cent, while the group describing themselves as 'mixed' had the youngest age structure – half were aged under 16 and just 4 per cent were aged 65 and over. In the white Irish population, one in four people was aged 65 and over (Office for National Statistics, 2005).

ACTIVITY **6.1**

List reasons that may account for the differences in demographic profile of the groups mentioned above.

Comment

Among the things you may have considered are that patterns of migration have an effect on the age range of people within a particular ethnic group.

Older migrants

As we have seen in the preceding chapters, there are few people in the world today who have not had some kind of experience of migration and its impact, including those in later life (Castles and Miller, 1998). Warnes, et al. (2004) undertook a study of older migrants, and concluded that *older migrants* include some of the most deprived and socially excluded, as well as some of the most affluent and accomplished – however, they are all to some extent disadvantaged. This occurs because of the interaction between social policies which tend to emphasis their *otherness* since they live in a foreign country. Thus, while older migrants have some things in common, there are significant differences in their experiences, which can be put down to their human capital. This means the extent to which they are prepared for old age.

Warnes and Williams (2006) have proposed a typology of older migrants, including affluent retirement migrants, labour migrants who have reached old age *in place* and *return migrants*. Below, we explore each of these categories and also consider a further group – those who migrate through necessity.

Affluent retirement migrants

As we saw in Chapter 2, 5.5 million people from the UK live permanently overseas, many having left to seek a warmer climate and better lifestyle, or to return to their country of birth. Affluent retired migrants in Europe migrate mainly from the north to the south with elders seeking a lifestyle change and an old age in the sun, particularly, though not exclusively, on the Spanish coasts and islands (Warnes, 2006). Such migration is often financed by accumulated wealth as a result of a positive educational experience, leading to stable employment, possibly a good occupational pension and the sale of a property. These relatively affluent migrants will typically have family or other social contacts they can call on at a distance for advice and support. If they are EU citizens, they will have access to state health care, or private health care facilities. However, they are unlikely to be able to call upon state domiciliary health or social care services, residential care or assisted housing as entitlement to such services does not normally extend beyond their home country. One example of voluntary organisations founded by expatriate communities to fill this gap and assist vulnerable or frail elders is *Age Concern España*, which was founded in 1994 and provides a range of services for British expatriates living in Spain, including an advice and information service, assistance for bereavement and financial hardship, and liaison with Spanish social services (Age Concern España, 2008). Another group of elders are those who migrate to be closer to family or friends, either within their own country or overseas. Over 820,000 UK elders receive their state pension overseas – nearly a quarter of those being in Australia and a significant number in the USA, Canada and the Irish Republic, as well as in the Southern Mediterranean (Warnes, 2006).

Labour migrants who have reached old age

Many people migrated overseas between the 1950s to the 1970s in search of employment and have subsequently *aged in place.* They were typically in their early working life and settled in new countries, either bringing their family with them at or after the time of migration, or bearing children in their destination country. They settled in communities with others of the same or similar ethnicities due to the availability of affordable housing, and some strong social networks were established. Many, although not all, entered low-skilled and manual work as they had comparatively little formal education and have experienced a lifetime of disadvantage including poor housing and health care and racial discrimination (Warnes, 2006). Others migrated during the period after the Second World War, responding to skills shortages. The National Health Service in the UK has always been highly dependent on doctors from India and migrant nurses from a variety of countries (Winkelmann-Gleed, 2006). Many of those early migrant doctors and nurses have *aged in place* and have now retired.

These labour migrants include some of the most socially excluded and disadvantaged elders in Western Europe (Warnes and Williams, 2006), and social workers can expect to work with some of these pioneer people.

Return migrants

Far less is known about the people who were long-term labour migrants who return to their country of origin when they retire from paid employment. They are socially, economically and ethnically diverse and move either from large cities to rural regions, or cross international borders to return 'home' (Warnes and Williams, 2006). Social workers are sometimes asked to assess and assist in requests by elders to 'return home', as we can read in the following case study.

CASE STUDY

Richard migrated to the UK from Kenya in the 1960s. He had steady employment and raised a family in Birmingham. In 1996 he suffered the first of a series of strokes which left him paralysed and speechless. He had been in a care home for nine years when he expressed a wish to return 'home' to Kenya for his remaining years.

Richard was referred by his social worker to International Social Services UK (ISS UK). The services provided by ISS UK include a Travel Assistance Programme that is statutorily funded by the Home Office. It assists those with settled status in the UK to return to their country of origin if they wish to do so. As well as administering the financial assistance scheme, ISS UK can provide an escort and in-country initial support if required, and can link the individual into appropriate services and support in their home country. Richard was found to meet the criteria for an assisted return under Section 58 of the 2002 Nationality, Immigration and Asylum Act and a member of his family was financially assisted to escort him 'home' and help settle him in. In a short time his health and well-being had significantly improved and he partially recovered some speech.

(Adapted from ISS UK, 2008)

Social workers need to be familiar with services and support available through recognised international agencies to enable referral in cases with international issues, such as the one outlined above.

Migration through necessity

As noted previously, some people migrate not as a matter of choice, but to flee war, famine, natural disaster, persecution or economic deprivation, seeking refuge in another country. In some cases, people may suffer post-traumatic stress disorder (PTSD) if they are from, for example, communities that have been affected by natural disaster or genocide (Lyons, et al., 2006). Social workers engaging with elders who have had such experiences either recently or in their past need to be aware that people from other cultures will interpret and understand such trauma in different ways. Knowledge of different theories that help guide assessment and intervention is crucial and Lyons, et al., argue that PTSD and trauma theories are highly relevant (2006, p66).

Understanding life's journeys

Journeys can refer to both geographical movement and pathways through the life course (see Chapter 1). Important factors which can determine how well people react to migration include someone's country of origin and pre-migration history; gender; their age when they migrated; the year or 'era' of their arrival; the place they settled in and any subsequent moves. All of these interact in complex ways and will all impact on their ability to change and adapt to another culture or to life's events (Burholt, 2004).

Transition and loss

Lyons, et al., describe loss as part of *a fundamental human experience that crosses borders, language, culture, age and social location* (2006, p64) and assert that social workers should be able to recognise, assess, and work with loss. Loss can be defined as the harm or suffering caused when someone loses someone or something. In later life, people will have experienced several layers of loss. These losses may include loss of country, culture, status, identity, as well as loved ones. They may also experience a loss of expectations and the reality of growing old in another country.

Grief, bereavement and mourning are terms that are often used interchangeably to describe how people deal with loss. The terms have different meanings: grief is a psychological reaction to loss; bereavement is a process that can accompany the loss of a loved person or object; and mourning is a public display of grief (Lyons, et al., 2006, p64). The way a person reacts to, expresses and deals with loss varies, depending upon personality, experience, education, class and belief system. Grief, bereavement and mourning are expressed differently in different cultures, but there are some general explanations of individual and social responses. Most cultures sanction crying, fear and anger within funeral rites and the customs associated with mourning, although in Western cultures the outward displays of emotion are not generally encouraged. The way people deal with and understand death is based upon cultural, traditional and/or religious belief systems, along with policy responses to the way a dying person or corpse is handled; thus, bereavement and mourning are *socially constructed*.

We can see this reflected in the way people of different religions and cultures deal with death and dying. Below are examples of mourning practices, which relate to long-standing and new migrant groups, but do read in more depth about some of the different cultural and religious practices around bereavement and funerals in the references given in the paragraphs below.

Eastern European

In the Russian Orthodox Church funeral arrangements are steeped in centuries of tradition, which are ingrained in the practices. In addition to the tradition of offering prayers for the deceased on the day of the funeral, it is also traditional to remember the deceased through prayers on the following dates: the third, ninth and the fortieth day after the date of the funeral.

Islam

Muslims see death as the end of the present life followed by a life hereafter. According to the Islamic faith, fellow human beings should be respected whether dead or alive and thus should be buried with respect and dignity according to their own faith and religious rites. Muslims are required to have their dead buried within a 24-hour period to ensure that the dead are laid to rest immediately and thereby relieved from any pain and suffering. There is great importance given to the duty of attending the funeral of the deceased, which is seen as an opportunity for mourners to show respect to the dead as well as gain reward and forgiveness for their own sins.

(Department of Health (DoH), 2004b; Advisory Conciliation and Arbitration Service (ACAS), 2005, pp37–50).

There are similarities and differences in practices around funeral arrangements and mourning and these illustrate the socially constructed nature of bereavement and mourning (Parkes, et al., 1997). It is important for social workers to be aware of such differences and show respect in such situations. There are a variety of theories concerning loss and grief, and an understanding of different cultural approaches can help social workers interpret and respond to people's needs in such situations (Lyons, et al., 2006). To understand the nature and meaning of loss, particularly for someone of a different culture, a life course perspective offers social workers a useful method for contextualising experiences.

A life course perspective

No one seeks social work help purely on the grounds of age – there is always another reason to do with physical or mental ill health, disability, restricted mobility, neglect or abuse or a particular social need. The tasks in working with elders are therefore similar to those in other areas of social work, namely: assessment, planning, intervention and review (Parker and Bradley, 2007).

Lymbery (2005) contends that the social work skills required in working with elders are equivalent to those needed in working with other service user and carer groups, and that an understanding of each older person's life experiences is essential. A life course perspective is especially useful when it involves a migratory experience. Crawford and Walker (2003, p3) define this perspective as *a viewpoint that considers the whole of life (from conception to death) as offering opportunities for growth, development and change*, and it:

- combines biological, sociological and psychological dimensions to give a holistic interpretation;

- draws on theories from a number of disciplines;

- is multidirectional – characterised by growth and loss with no one pathway seen as 'normal';

- is influenced by a person's life history, socio-cultural and socio-economic conditions;

- is contextual – influenced by the person, their reactions and the context in which they live their lives.

It is important to listen to the service user's 'story' or biographical details to understand the context to their current situation and to plan from there. Taking this type of narrative approach is helpful in appreciating how people can respond to situations differently, based on the meanings and influences that have shaped their lives. These will include their personal history, ethnicity and culture, individual characteristics and psychosocial circumstances (Crawford and Walker, 2004, p11).

Social professionals have become increasingly aware that the elder population is becoming both ethnically and culturally more diverse. For example, those people who have recently migrated may experience considerable health and social problems. In the UK, the National Service Framework for Older People (DoH, 2001) requires services to *recognise individual differences and specific needs including cultural and religious difference* (p23). This is a policy response to the impact of globalisation and migration and its effect upon an individual over their life course. Individuals will have gained both strengths and vulnerabilities from their experiences and will need a personalised response to any plans and support they may require for the future.

It would be wrong always to assume that elders from other cultures have lower life satisfaction or levels of support than the majority population. Levels of self-esteem and a strong identity across the life course can be the result of having a distinctive cultural or ethnic heritage (Blakemore and Boneham, 1994). Some elders who have migrated to a country may have aspirations about 'returning home' or renewing contacts and it is sometimes appropriate to discuss expectations and the strength of any contacts with family and friends and the levels of support that may be available.

CASE STUDY

Sophia, a 72-year-old woman, originally from Jamaica, has care needs because of restricted mobility due to Parkinson's disease. She lives alone following the death of her husband four years ago. She still manages to walk slowly and spends time with friends from her local church and others who own local shops. Her GP referred her to social services for help with walking aids and adaptations to her home. During her initial assessment, Sophia says she does not want to attend a local day centre for lunches as it is only 'for white people'. She also mentions that she has a sister in Jamaica but says she lost contact with her some time ago, as her husband did not get on with her during a visit by her sister to England. She would like to be able to get in touch with her sister again, but does not know where she lives now.

Comment

Sophia has suffered losses of several kinds (country, spouse, sister, mobility) and this should be a feature of her assessment (see discussion above).

Listening to Sophia's life story and discussing the reasons she lost contact with her sister would help clarify for Sophia how resuming contact might best be achieved. If Sophia still wants to resume contact, then a referral to the International Social Service UK Tracing Service should be considered (www.issuk.org.uk). The ISS UK Tracing Service helps people in the UK contact relatives abroad and also helps people overseas contact relatives in the UK. ISS UK only use public records and conduct such searches sensitively, to avoid shocks or unpleasant surprises.

Sometimes social workers have made assumptions that elders from minority ethnic groups have supportive kinship networks. This has sometimes been used as an excuse to either refuse or delay provision which they, as members of the community, could have expected to receive. It would be good practice to check that local provision is appropriate to the needs of all in the community and to audit local provision to check exactly what is available in order to present Sophia with real choices.

Attitudes and ageism

Elders often face discrimination solely on the grounds of their age. In very traditional societies and in many religious groups, elders are respected and enjoy a high status. The elders of the community are seen as having the wisdom that comes with age and experience and the younger generation seek their views on a variety of issues. The same is true of some sectors or classes of society in more developed countries. Judges, politicians and senior directors or executives are seldom subject to the norms of retirement that are common to other occupations. Indeed, in some countries it seems a positive advantage for politicians to be in their eighties, notably in China and some of the African states.

However, this is not always the case and many elders experience a very low status in their society, often accompanied by increasing poverty as they reach very old age. In other words, they experience ageism. Put very simply, ageism is the oppression of people solely on the grounds of their age, just as racism and sexism discriminate on the grounds of ethnicity and gender (Bytheway, 1995).

ACTIVITY 6.2

Make two lists of words used to describe elders – one negative, one positive.

Comment

Some of the language often used to refer to elders can convey respect and a notion of the person having wisdom; some terms imply that people have rights; and some terms are discriminatory and imply that elders are a homogeneous group of people indistinguishable from each other and largely redundant.

Ageism differs from other oppressions in that we will all be old some day, barring an early death, whereas the white racist will never be black nor the male sexist a woman. There is a difference between age discrimination and ageism, the oppression of elders. During our lives, we all experience age discrimination of various sorts where policies state that age should determine when we are able to do certain things – for example, the age at which we can begin and leave compulsory schooling; when we can have sexual relations; when we can drive, smoke or drink alcohol; the age at which we acquire criminal responsibility; and the age at which we are entitled to a pension. However, in many societies, *ageist* attitudes and values have become part of the rules that govern many of our institutions and social life. They blend so imperceptibly into everyday values and attitudes that they have a drastic effect on the way elders live their lives and are viewed by others. This is what is known as institutional or structural ageism.

Blakemore and Boneham (1994, p40) point to the *combined impact of race, age and social class* or *multiple hazard* on the lives of elders from minority ethnic groups in diverse, modern societies, which is in addition to the ageism faced by the majority elder population. They also point to the strengths and satisfaction some elders gain from their strong cultural heritage and the resulting contribution they can make to their host society.

Cultural understandings of ageing well

It is important to remember that many elders live full and satisfying lives, and many are engaged in intergenerational activities by providing care for siblings, friends, children, grandchildren, groups and communities. Avramov and Maskova (2003) refer to the concept of *active ageing* or the involvement by elders in the different domains of their personal, family, social and professional life. Active ageing incorporates an individualised mix of activities in:

- employment;
- domestic work and care (paid and unpaid);
- community engagement, including voluntary work;
- leisure activities (e.g. sports, travel, creative activities).

Avramov and Maskova (2003), writing from a European perspective, point to the detrimental effects of inactive ageing that can include loss of income and too much time spent on passive home-centred leisure that can lead to isolation, depression and a poorer quality of life. The Iranian concept of ageing well, on the other hand, equates successful ageing with growing dignified and leading a slower, more passive and disengaged life at leisure and being dependent on younger generations of the family (Torres, 2006, p131). A cross-cultural perspective is essential to understand a person's approach to later life and the potential for actions and lifestyle being misunderstood. Community profiling and strengthening of social networks are important activities for social workers engaging with all elders. Connectedness with others who share life experiences or understand cultural heritage helps alleviate the feelings of loss of home and heritage, particularly for elders from minority ethnic groups.

People who have experienced a lifetime of deprivation and/or loss are less likely to have the social capital that is required for a fulfilling and healthy old age and their engagement with the labour market may well be of necessity due to a low income and poverty.

Incomes, pensions and poverty

The type of work and employment pattern that people have during their working lives largely determines the size of a person's income during retirement. In the more developed countries, many people receive their income from employment or self-employment until they are into their fifties or sixties. By the time people are in their seventies, however, elders receive part of their income via state benefits of different kinds, probably including some form of state retirement pension. In addition to this, an increasing number of people also have income from private or occupational pensions. This is affected by an individual's life course work pattern, so people with broken work records will have accrued a lower level of state, private or occupational pension (Phillips et al., 2006; Office for National Statistics, 2005).

ACTIVITY **6.3**

Think about reasons why people might have lower paid and less secure employment. Make a list of the groups that are more likely to be affected by these factors.

Comment

Among the groups you may have listed might be women, who often take career breaks when having families or to take on caring tasks. Unskilled workers are another group who are more vulnerable to unstable employment and their pension rights will therefore be affected. People from minority ethnic groups are often affected by insecure or short-term employment, because of the processes of migration and discrimination and are less likely to obtain secure, well-paid positions. This results in a reduced income in their later life.

Learning from patterns of welfare in other countries

In developed countries worldwide, the move away from institutional care for vulnerable elders has been an observable trend. Different approaches and strategies have been developed to facilitate care in the community, resource rationing and cost-shifting from the state to individuals and families (Hokenstad and Midgley, 1997). The nature of policies and approaches to community-based care is largely dependent on the history of welfare, the values and the culture of each society. Policy will reflect the level of responsibility placed on families to care for their elders; expectations about whether women should be in paid employment; housing and employment opportunities – enabling families to remain geographically close, or requiring people to move away for work or housing. It will also reflect the availability of carers (whether voluntary or paid) and the profile of the care sector workforce. In any discussion about service provision, it is worth remembering that elders from minority groups often do not have equal access to social, health and economic services compared to the majority population (Crawford and Walker, 2004).

In line with the policies of deinstitutionalisation, most people over 65 years old live in the community, either with another person, their extended family or, increasingly, alone (Crawford and Walker, 2004, p28). Elders may enjoy companionship and support from a social network consisting of their family members, friends, neighbours and clubs or organisations of different sorts. Most elders who need assistance with daily living receive it from some of the people in their social network and do not require additional help from social care services and this is known as informal care.

Home care

For people who do not have access to informal care, or need a greater level of care than can be provided informally, care can be provided by social care agencies within the community either in the person's own home (domiciliary provision) or in a centre within the local community. This type of care is given to enable people to live interdependently rather than going into some form of supported accommodation. Social care for elders can be provided by the state, voluntary or charitable agencies or by private for-profit organisations. We can gain useful insights, comparisons and innovative ideas by looking at provision locally, nationally and internationally.

RESEARCH SUMMARY

Social workers in the Italian city of Parma developed a system that put elders at the centre of the care process. A local network of agencies providing home care, safe at home support services, home counselling and assisted holidays were offered contracts based on a fixed price. This was to avoid competition based on cost, which might have compromised quality. Service contracts were offered and an accreditation system was developed with the elder and their family providing the evaluations. Social workers help devise individualised care plans and give the elder vouchers that they can use to purchase care from an accredited provider, in line with the care plan. The strong consensus on the importance of social services results in 30 per cent of the local authority budget funding a high level of service.

One type of agency that has proven very popular is the social co-operative. This broadens the concept of a voluntary organisation by integrating volunteers from socially excluded and disadvantaged groups to provide care and welfare services. The social co-operatives in Italy are local non-profit organisations that receive grants from the government towards running costs.

(Campanini, 2007; Bonnetti and Manfredi, 2007)

Comment

The voluntary sector or non-governmental organisations (NGOs) are increasingly providing home care services by being contracted by the state sector in many countries. Some advantages of using NGOs are that they may be closer to the needs of the service users; they may have more autonomy from political influence, being partly funded by voluntary donations; and they can be a source of innovation. A disadvantage for NGOs is that through the contract they can lose some of their autonomy as they are obliged to provide services to given specifications.

Supported housing

As with other forms of care, supported housing can be provided by the state, voluntary or private sectors. Supported housing usually comprises self-contained accommodation such as a house, bungalow or apartment in an estate or block, with on-site support given by a caretaker, warden, housekeeper or social care staff for people who do not need residential care, but who no longer wish to live unsupported. Sometimes communal services, such as laundry or social spaces are provided as well as home care services, such as cleaning and shopping and communal meals. Services in private facilities can be expensive and residents often pay a standard service charge yearly for on-site support. State and voluntary sector provision is often means-tested in the UK.

Gated communities exclusively for elders are proliferating, largely for the wealthier in the population in many developed countries, notably the USA. Many residents move to such communities out of a fear of crime or perceived lack of stability of their locality. Gated communities have their own shops, entertainment and facilities, within a walled area with security surveillance. The major disadvantage of such communities is that they can deprive whole areas of elders who could otherwise make a real contribution to their neighbourhood and are seen by some as being very socially divisive (Price and Simpson, 2007, p135).

ACTIVITY **6.4**

Who provides supported housing for elders in your locality? Is it state, voluntary or private provision? Who is the provision for? Does it cater for all elders?

Comment

Along with general social housing, supported housing is increasingly provided by NGOs such as housing associations, or the private sector. While it offers people a level of independence when they need additional support with daily living, the main disadvantage is that elders often have to move away from local friends for such provision and the neighbourhood they leave loses its elder citizens.

RESEARCH SUMMARY

In France, a group of researchers had observed that there were many elders living in large old apartment blocks, some having been built hundreds of years ago, in many towns and cities. The elders sometimes included people from different ethnicities, who were part of very well-established communities. As some of the elders became frail or ill and were unable to cope with daily living they often went into either hospital or residential care. Others became isolated as friends and neighbours died and families moved away. Most of the elders had expressed a desire to remain in their community, having lived there for a great part, if not all, of their lives.

The solution found was a form of provision known as the domicile collectif *(collective residence), the first opening in 1988. Several ground-floor apartments in a block were joined and adapted into interconnected studios for people needing varying levels of care.*

RESEARCH SUMMARY *continued*

The different professionals and workers who had been visiting the elders separately were put on to a 24-hour rota to provide continuous specialist assistance. The teams comprised nurses, doctors, social work and social care staff, physiotherapists, occupational therapists, psychologists. The outcome for the residents was that they were able to remain in their own community for the remainder of their lives, having the benefit of continuing contact with their friends and family.

See, for example: Centre du Rhône d'Information et d'Action Sociale en faveur des retraités et des personnes âgées *(CRIAS) (2008);* Domicile collectif Nantes et communauté urbaine (2008); Centre Pluridisciplinaire de Gérontologie *(CPDG) (2008).*

Residential care

Despite the trend towards community care in many parts of the world, some people require extended care in a supported environment. It is difficult to compare accurately the numbers of people living in residential care in different countries as the supply of care facilities and the policy on care in part determines demand. Numbers in residential care tell us more about government policy than choice or preference of elders. Types of residential care home vary, from establishments where residents require limited amounts of care, to nursing homes that provide extended care for people with high levels of need arising from physical or mental ill health. The quality of residential care for elders also varies from inclusive, engaging and very comfortable facilities at one extreme to very large institutional establishments that are little more than 'people warehouses' at the other extreme. As with other provision, care homes can be provided by the state, voluntary (NGOs) or private sectors, depending upon state policy around provision of care (Hugman, 1994; Walker and Maltby, 1997).

Working with elders: A gendered and international workforce

Social work and social care with elders holds all of the challenges and rewards of working with people of other ages and they need a workforce that reflects the diversity in communities. In the UK some authorities and agencies have trainee schemes aimed at particular minorities who are under-represented. Some authorities also actively recruit social workers from other countries and the General Social Care Council (GSCC) reported that 4,808 out of 70,000 registered social workers were trained overseas in 2005–6 (GSCC, 2007).

It is not always qualified social workers who work with elders. Paid carers include care managers, social care workers, domiciliary care workers and home carers, who all provide services of differing kinds. In the UK, care managers can hold one of a variety of qualifications, or sometimes not have formal qualifications. However, the majority of people caring for elders are informal carers. Families have traditionally provided care, but families today are more prone to dispersal due to globalisation, worker mobility and housing policies. This has meant that many people – especially women – struggle to balance the needs of a vulnerable relative or friend with the requirements of work, their own family, or their own ageing (Crawford and Walker, 2004).

Due to its low pay and low status, care work with elders in the UK is often performed by people who find difficulty in gaining better paid employment for a variety of reasons. Women and members of minority ethnic groups comprise the majority of this workforce (Price and Simpson, 2007, pp84–5). This contact between people from minority ethnic groups and elders from the majority population (who have perhaps lived their lives with little such contact) can result in tensions.

ACTIVITY **6.5**

Ethel, an older frail woman, has made racist comments to Constance, a care worker originally from Zimbabwe. What might Ethel's social worker do in this situation?

Comment

The social worker would need to discuss with Ethel the effect of her comments on Constance and why this is not acceptable. The social worker would need to listen to Ethel's account of events to decide how best to handle the situation. Ethel might not understand that what she is saying is racist, or it may be that Ethel does hold racist views, in which case the social worker would have to explain her agency policy to prevent Constance from having to deal with racist remarks. Anti-oppressive practice in social work with elders can be highly challenging since their attitudes will reflect the life course they have experienced.

C H A P T E R   S U M M A R Y

In this chapter we have considered some international aspects of social work with elders and the effects of globalisation. This requires social workers to have knowledge of the different contexts for social work with elders in and beyond the UK. Social workers need skills in working with elders from and between different countries, cultures and minority groups, values which respect difference and promote the principles of human rights and social justice for elders.

FURTHER READING

Daatland, S and Biggs, S (2006) *Ageing and diversity*. Bristol: Policy Press.
The editors have used material from theory, original research and empirical studies to address stereotypes of ageing and explore the meaning of diversity in the context of later life.

Lyons, K, Manion, C and Carlsen, M (2006) *International perspectives of social work*. Basingstoke: Palgrave Macmillan.
This is a very accessible book that addresses international issues from a thematic perspective. See particularly Chapter 4, 'Loss: A core concept with universal relevance' that discusses the relationship between globalisation and loss.

Chapter 7

International aspects of social work with people with disabilities

Vicky Price and Nathalie Huegler

This chapter will enable you to become familiar with the following National Occupational Standards for Social Work.

Key Role 2: Plan, carry out, review and evaluate social work practice, with individuals, families, carers, groups, communities and other professionals.

5.3 Apply and justify social work methods and models used to achieve change and development, and to improve life opportunities.

Key Role 3: Support individuals to represent their needs, views and circumstances.

10.2 Assist individuals, families, carers, groups and communities to access independent advocacy.

10.3 Advocate for, and with, individuals, families, carers, groups and communities.

Key Role 6: Demonstrate professional competence in social work practice.

18.1 Review and update your own knowledge of legal, policy and procedural frameworks.

20.1 Identify and assess issues, dilemmas and conflicts that might affect your practice.

20.2 Devise strategies to deal with ethical issues, dilemmas and conflicts.

It will also introduce you to the following academic standards set out in the 2008 Quality Assurance Agency social work subject benchmark statement.

4. Defining principles.

4.3 (...) Social work is located within different social welfare contexts.

Within the UK there are different traditions of social welfare (influenced by legislation, historical development and social attitudes) and these have shaped both social work education and practice in community-based settings including residential, day care and substitute care. In an international context, distinctive national approaches to social welfare policy, provision and practice have greatly influenced the focus and content of social work degree programmes.

5.1.1 Social work services, service users and carers.

- the social processes (associated with, for example, poverty, migration, unemployment, poor health, disablement, lack of education and other sources of disadvantage) that lead to marginalisation, isolation and exclusion, and their impact on the demand for social work services;
- explanations of the links between definitional processes contributing to social differences (for example, social class, gender, ethnic differences, age, sexuality and religious belief) and the problems of inequality and differential need faced by service users.
- the nature of social work services in a diverse society (with particular reference to concepts such as prejudice, interpersonal, institutional and structural discrimination, empowerment and anti-discriminatory practices);

- the nature and validity of different definitions of, and explanations for, the characteristics and circumstances of service users and the services required by them, drawing on knowledge from research, practice experience, and from service users and carers;
- the focus on outcomes, such as promoting the well-being of young people and their families, and promoting dignity, choice and independence for adults receiving services.

5.1.2 The service delivery context.

- the location of contemporary social work within historical, comparative and global perspectives, including European and international contexts;
- the changing demography and cultures of communities in which social workers will be practising;
- the significance of legislative and legal frameworks and service delivery standards (including the nature of legal authority, the application of legislation in practice, statutory accountability and tensions between statute, policy and practice).

5.1.3 Values and ethics.

- the complex relationships between justice, care and control in social welfare and the practical and ethical implications of these, including roles as statutory agents and in upholding the law in respect of discrimination.

5.1.4 Social work theory.

- the relevance of sociological perspectives to understanding societal and structural influences on human behaviour at individual, group and community levels;
- the relevance of psychological, physical and physiological perspectives to understanding personal and social development and functioning;
- user-led perspectives.

5.1.5 The nature of social work practice.

- the processes that facilitate and support service user choice and independence;
- the place of theoretical perspectives and evidence from international research in assessment and decision-making processes in social work practice;
- the integration of theoretical perspectives and evidence from international research into the design and implementation of effective social work intervention, with a wide range of service users, carers and others.

Introduction

Previous chapters have explored aspects of international social work in relation to service user groups, and this chapter continues that theme in relation to disabled people. The nature of disability is diverse: some people are born with an impairment (for example, Down's syndrome); others become impaired because of an acute illness (for example, polio); for others it is as a result of an accident; for some it is due to illness or disease associated with the ageing process; for others it is related to mental ill health. As we will discuss further on in the chapter, some people see the impairment as being the disability, while for others it is society which 'disables'. The World Health Organisation (WHO) lists the main causes of disability globally as:

- chronic diseases (including diabetes, cardiovascular diseases and cancer);

- injuries (such as road traffic accidents, the consequences of war, including injuries to the civilian population through land-mines);

- mental impairments;

- birth defects;

- malnutrition.

(WHO, 2006)

A central factor influencing the situation of disabled people is the response of society. Therefore, considering disability from an international perspective means looking at:

- a complex interplay of different societies' and cultures' responses to a range of 'disabilities' or 'impairments';

- how these responses are affected by international organisations and aspects of globalisation;

- the experiences of disabled people themselves.

The chapter will look at disability from an international perspective in a number of ways. First, it looks at the extent of disability in a global context; second, it shows how our understanding of disability has been influenced by international writers and campaigners; third, it shows how key policy features of adult social care in the UK reflect developments in other countries. In particular, the personalisation agenda (Department of Health, 2007), based on the idea that service users should have maximum choice in the support or care they receive, rather than having to fit in with available services, is not just 'local' to the UK, but has global dimensions.

In previous chapters a theme has been developed around how the global movement of people – migration – creates new challenges for social workers in the UK specifically (and the developed 'North' in general), and this theme will be continued in the later sections of this chapter, before concluding with some ideas of how an international perspective can help our understanding. Before we can do any of this, however, we need to come to an understanding of what we mean by the terms 'disability' and 'disabled people'.

ACTIVITY 7.1

Spend some time thinking about how you would define the term 'disability'.

Comment

Probably most of you will have thought about specific disabling conditions and, more than likely, some of you will have identified society as being a key 'disabling factor' – following what has come to be known as the 'social model of disability' (Oliver, 1990; Morris, 1991). Defining disability in an international context is, however, more complex.

Different countries have different types of definitions. Many of these are legal definitions based on medical understandings of disability. For example, the 1995 Disability Discrimination Act in the UK defined disability as:

> *a physical, or mental impairment which has a substantial and long-term*
> *adverse effect on a person's ability to carry out normal day-to-day activities.*
> (Disability Discrimination Act 1995, s 1(1))

The Disability Discrimination Act of 2005 extended this definition to include people with specific conditions – cancer, HIV infection or multiple sclerosis – as having a disability from the day of diagnosis, rather than waiting until the condition has an impact on their ability to carry out 'day-to-day activities'. The Act also provides more detailed guidance listed below, on the terms used in the definition of 'disability'.

- Substantial means neither minor nor trivial.

- Long-term means that the impairment has lasted, or is likely to last, for 12 months. (There are specific provisions for recurring impairments.)

- Normal day-to-day activities include eating, washing, walking and going shopping and these must affect a capacity identified in the Act such as mobility, manual dexterity, speech, hearing, seeing and memory.

(DirectGov, 2008)

In Germany, however, the legal definition sets shorter time-scales (six months) and allows for an earlier acceptance of disability through anticipation of the effects of a particular impairment, according to guidance issued in 2001 (German Ninth book of the social law code – 'Sozialgesetzbuch IX').

Just by comparing two EU member states, we can see differences in legal definitions. However, the wide range of definitions of disability becomes even clearer when we look at international non-governmental organisations. To conclude the discussion about definitions, we now turn to Disabled People's International (DPI), a network of organisations or assemblies of disabled people. For many years, DPI did not use a specific definition, citing the following reasons in a position paper:

- legislation in different countries uses a variety of definitions;

- most of the definitions used are based on a medical understanding of disability;

- the definitions used in different countries are often difficult to translate;

- some countries use terms which in other countries are considered unacceptable.

(DPI, 2005)

As a result, DPI member organisations and independent NGOs used their own definitions, leading to a wide range of understandings of the term 'disability'. In 2005, following wide consultation seeking the views of disabled people, the organisation adopted the following definition:

> *The International Classification of Functioning (ICF) defines disability as the outcome of the interaction between a person with an impairment and the environmental and attitudinal barriers he/she may face.*

(DPI, 2005)

ACTIVITY 7.2

Think about how and why the above definition differs from the definitions in UK legislation.

Comment

DPI is an international organisation which is made up of disabled people (rather than politicians who have to work through the policy implications of legislation). It is therefore an international pressure group, whose work seeks to influence governments around the world. The definition adopted by DPI does not identify any specific impairments, nor does it set time-scales or use the concept of 'normal day-to-day activities'. The most important difference from the earlier mentioned legal definitions is the argument that disability is an interaction between the 'impairment' and environmental and/or attitudinal barriers disabled people face. This is something that we will continue to consider during the rest of the chapter.

Factors concerning the extent of disability

In the UK, estimates of the numbers of disabled people vary. According to the Disability Rights Commission (DRC) there were 11 million disabled people in the UK in 2005, around one in five of the population (DRC, 2005, p7). An earlier large-scale survey taken between 1985–88 set the figure at 14.2 per cent of the *adult* population. This survey, the last of its kind, was highly criticised by disabled people, and formed the basis of Michael Oliver's (1990) critiques, since its focus was on the impairments and not on the disabling barriers in society. Oliver proposed alternative questions: for example, instead of gathering data on whether children attended special schools due to long-term health problems or disabilities, the focus was on local authorities' education policies.

The numbers of disabled people worldwide are estimated at 650 million or around 10 per cent of the world's population. The vast majority (80 per cent) are thought to be living in developing countries (International Labour Organization (ILO), 2007). We should remember that in a global context many people are disabled as a consequence of war – including large numbers of civilians. At the same time, people with disabilities can also be particularly vulnerable in situations of forced displacement through conflicts and violence, and their needs are often neglected in existing support programmes for refugees (Women's Commission for Refugee Women and Children (WCRWC), 2008). Although systematically collected data is not available, it is estimated that between 3 per cent and 10 per cent of refugees and asylum seekers living in the UK have a disability – and many experience particular problems in accessing appropriate support, not least due to language barriers and restrictions on their welfare entitlements as a result of their immigration status (Roberts and Harris, 2002).

The work of the WHO in relation to disability on a global level is to promote the health and rehabilitation of disabled people, enhance public health programmes (something often taken for granted in rich countries) and raise awareness of disability 'issues' (WHO, 2008c). The WHO seeks to promote improvements in opportunities for disabled people at regional, national and global levels. The disability action plan (WHO, 2006) states that the number of people with disabilities is increasing because of:

- population growth;
- ageing;
- chronic diseases;
- medical advances which prolong life.

Poverty is often a key contributory factor to the *extent* of disability, for example, poorer people are more likely to contract chronic disease through lack of adequate clean water and food, and they are also more often displaced as a result of conflicts. Poverty is also a *consequence* and *experience* of disability, as we will see when considering the position of disabled people and work.

Understanding disability

There are, as we have already noted, different ways of defining disability and these stem from different ways of understanding disability. The development of the social model of disability in the 1990s was highly influential. One of the key writers in this field is Michael Oliver, whom we mentioned in the last section when introducing a key aspect of the social model: the fact that, rather than emphasising the disabling nature of the impairment, it emphasises the disabling nature of society. Society disables people with a range of impairments in relation to, for example, common 'assumptions' held about them, the use of language, or the design of the built environment (limiting access). In this way, it is argued, society erects disabling barriers (for an early account see Swain, et al., 1993; or Barnes et al., 1999 for a fuller exposition of disability theory). In essence, the model argues that as disabled people are full citizens, they should be able to realise their full citizenship rights. Legislation in many countries has included anti-discriminatory aspects, and the UK's Disability Discrimination Acts of 1995 and 2005 are good examples of this. International organisations also seek to promote disabled people's rights at both national and international levels, as we have seen earlier in the chapter.

The social model was developed as a critique of existing ways of seeing disability. The previously mentioned large-scale survey in the UK was a good example of how disability was 'constructed' by those who were researching its extent. This type of construction, which focused on the impairment, to the exclusion of societal factors, became known as 'the medical model'. This does not mean that disability rights activists and writers necessarily argue against medical interventions (though there are some who hold this position). Rather, they oppose the medicalisation of disability, which ignores the social aspect and portrays disabled people as either 'tragic victims' or 'heroic strugglers' (Barnes *et al.*, 1999). This almost exclusive focus of the medical model on the impairment fails to fully consider the person and their experiences of how impairment and environment interact.

Within the field of learning disability, the normalisation movement has had a great influence on service provision. The main people associated with this movement are the Canadian Wolf Wolfensberger and the Swede Bengt Nirje. Nirje formulated his views after working with refugees following the Second World War and he was also influenced by some of John Bowlby's work in relation to institutions. In his work with people with learning disabilities, he collaborated with other Scandinavian academics and activists. Wolfensberger, who developed the ideas more fully, was highly influenced by Nirje's work (Race, 2003). Nirje (1969) formulated a set of key principles for the normalisation of people with learning disabilities and these included: a normal rhythm of the day, and of the year (this includes holidays and family life celebrations); a normal pattern of living, going to various leisure facilities and not having them all in one place; experiencing a 'normal education'; no segregation of men and women (as was common in many institutions); economic independence; and the same right of access to social institutions – for example, schools and hospitals. The impact of these ideas in the 1960s could be described as 'revolutionary' even if they seem relatively 'standard' in many Northern countries today. Although the concept of normalisation has also been subjected to various critiques, it has remained as a key model for the development of services for people with learning disabilities, and has been followed in Scandinavia and parts of North America since the 1960s and 1970s (Race, 2003). Nirje was also involved with parents movements, which were dominant in post-war Germany, and adopted some of the Swedish ideas into the concept of *Lebenshilfe* (help for living). This was seen as a viable alternative to, and critique of, church-based institutions (Schädler, et al., 2004).

Oliver (1999) critiques normalisation from a social model perspective, arguing that it fails to take account of the structural socio-economic conditions which create oppression of disabled people, and therefore cannot transform their lives. Race, et al. (2005), on the other hand, note that 'normalisation' (or 'social role valorisation', as it became known) has improved services in many countries and underpins much of UK policy for people with learning disabilities, although this is not explicitly acknowledged. Despite the continuing debate between the two perspectives of 'normalisation' and the social model, the authors argue that both models emanate from the experiences of oppressed people and therefore share much common ground. The extent to which the ideas have shaped policy can be seen in the response of the Scottish Disability Equality Forum (SDEF) to the Scottish Government's 2007 budget. The SDEF pointed out that it was

> ... *pleased to see that the Committee has recommended the adoption of the social model of disability in terms of recognising the external barriers that are disabling. However, there is merit in considering the ongoing debate of the social model rather than seeing disability in an overly simplistic manner.*
>
> (SDEF, 2007)

Both Race, et al. (2005) and Shakespeare (2006) identify difficulties which arise when relying solely on the 'social model' approach. Shakespeare argues that a problematic polarisation has emerged between 'medical' and 'social' models, connected with a focus on either 'impairment' or 'disability'. The debates on these issues might seem to be mainly 'academic' or 'intellectual', but they do in fact have a direct impact on the lives of disabled people. Within the UK context, where the social model is dominant within both social work and current social policy discourses, Shakespeare's critique is particularly relevant. For example, he draws attention to the social model's claim that disability can be removed by social change, and to the fact that this plays down the role of impairments in people's lives (Shakespeare, 2006, p52).

Shakespeare argues that 'disability' is not, nor can be, an all-embracing term, and that the social model has served people with learning disabilities or intellectual impairments less well than physically impaired people. Shakespeare's main point is that the debate between models fails to take account of the experiences of disabled people, who just *want to be seen as ordinary members of society, free of limitation or classification* (2006, p72). Shakespeare's views are controversial, but his position is, interestingly, very much in tune with the earlier mentioned definition which DPI has adopted – emphasising that both the *nature of the impairment* and the *response of other people to it* (environmental and attitudinal) are significant in understanding disability fully.

Linked to Shakespeare's critique of the social model is the question of identity. One of the consequences of the social model, he argues, is that in emphasising the need to create a disabled identity, alliances with non-disabled people are questioned.

The theme of *negotiating identities* has been explored by Zoebia Islam, in the context of her research among Pakistani and Bangladeshi young disabled people (2008). The following summary of her research demonstrates how people's experiences are influenced by cultural diversity in societies (a main aspect of this book's recurring theme of the presence of the 'global' in local settings).

RESEARCH SUMMARY

Islam, Z (2008) Negotiating identities: The lives of Pakistani and Bangladeshi young disabled people

The social model emphasises that disability is socially constructed and that developing a disabled identity is important as the first stage of empowerment. Critics of this position argue that this has the potential to reduce people's identities exclusively to being disabled and fails to acknowledge the multifaceted nature of identity. Islam carried out research among Bangladeshi and Pakistani young people who were disabled and demonstrated how they negotiated different aspects of their identity, notably ethnicity, religion, 'race' and gender as well as disability. Most young people referred to 'disability' as their actual impairment and some positively utilised it, for example by paying reduced admission prices at the cinema.

They also showed how other people's attitudes created difficulties for them: for example being stared at in public places, or being ignored in conversations when people addressed their parents and not them directly. Others were very much aware of how society created barriers for them, especially in future employment opportunities. Most of the young people saw themselves as belonging to a non-British culture and having to negotiate this in their daily lives, although not all of the young people identified with their parents' religious attitudes. One of the findings was that disabled Pakistani and Bangladeshi young people in the study would not only make alliances with other disabled people (who may be from outside their ethnic group), but would also join non-disabled people within their ethnic group to combat aspects of racism they experienced in British society.

The impact of disability

We have looked at definitions and models for understanding disability, many of which have been developed by disabled people. However, often ideas and models can seem abstract – and we therefore now turn to exploring the impact of being disabled, and also look at how disabled people have engaged in self-advocacy to combat discrimination at all levels.

Education

We begin with a short journey back into history, when disabled people were routinely placed in institutions for either their entire life or for a period of education. The institutions were not only highly controlling, but also segregating; and often people were sent there against their own and their families' wishes (Hreinsdóttir, et al., 2006).

Mary's story

Mary was born in 1923. She had a dislocated hip and walked with a limp. She had three brothers and her father was wounded in the First World War. When her mother died in 1933, the authorities considered her father unable to bring up the children on his own. Mary and her brothers were sent to the workhouse. Until 1948, when welfare reforms abolished workhouses, poor people in England were often sent to these large institutions. From the workhouse, Mary was separated from the rest of her family, and sent to a special institutional school for girls who had physical or learning disabilities. When she arrived at the institution, she had her hair cut short, and was bathed and scrubbed with carbolic soap. She began to cry and was rubbed down with rough towels and told to stop. The next day she was given a number which she kept during her time in the institution. She later said that she had entered into a different life: ... I thought everyone had forsaken me ... Our lockers in the playroom had the same number and our clothes were marked with our numbers so we knew what we had ... we never had names we were just numbers there.

(Adapted from Humphries and Gordon, 1992, pp68–69)

Experiences such as Mary's were commonplace and continued with institutional provision for education until relatively recently. Indeed, segregated and institutional educational provision still continues in the UK and in many other countries. Many people, however, were not placed into institutions, but remained with their families (Rolph, et al., 2005). Rolph, et al. (2003) wrote about the actions of social workers employed as mental welfare officers in East Anglia, whose role included educating parents in how to look after their learning disabled children. However, many of the social workers interviewed said that, apart from visiting, nothing much was done, and that many families lived with the fear that their children would be removed and placed in an institution – something which often happened when the parents died. Inclusive education is now a United Nations objective and a recent report of the United Nations Educational, Scientific and Cultural Organisation (UNESCO), monitoring progress towards fully inclusive education worldwide by 2015, makes the following comment:

> *There is increasing recognition, especially in Europe, that it is preferable for children with special needs to be taught in regular schools, albeit with various forms of special support. In recent years several developing countries have taken initiatives to promote inclusive schools. In Brazil, the 2002 Education Law emphasizes the need for schools to promote enrolment of children with specific learning needs and commits the government to providing specialized teachers. Ethiopia's special education needs strategy, introduced in 2006, is designed to encourage inclusive schooling by training teachers to identify learning difficulties and to establish support systems.*

(UNESCO, 2007 p27)

Try and find out what the arrangements are in your area for the education of children with special needs.

Comment

What you discover will vary considerably as to where you live; this will not just relate to the country you live in, but also the local area. In 2003, there were around 250,000 pupils with a Statement of Special Educational Needs in England (this does not, however, equate to the number of pupils with a disability, since many children are not 'statemented' – depending, again, on local factors). Of these, 63 per cent were in mainstream schools, and 37 per cent in special schools or pupil referral units – meaning that just under four out of every ten disabled children were likely to be educated in some form of segregated provision (Office for National Statistics (ONS), 2004). Sweden has a higher level of integration, although special schools do exist for children in the following groups: visual impairment combined with additional disabilities; deafness or hearing impairment combined with learning disabilities, or congenital deaf-blindness respectively; severe speech and language disorder (*Special pedagogiska skol myndigheten* (SPSM), 2008).

Education plays a vital role for many disabled people as it impacts on their future life chances. Education is also a determining factor for employment opportunities, which for disabled people are likely to be greatly reduced as a result of widespread discrimination – despite legislation making this illegal.

Employment

In the UK, 50 per cent of people with disabilities were in paid employment in 2006, compared to over 80 per cent of those without a disability. Disabled people were three times more likely to be economically inactive but people with a disability were more likely to want a job (Disability Rights Commission, 2007). In Europe, according to a report by the ILO (2007, pp44–45), the overall chance of a person aged between 16 and 64 finding employment is estimated at 66 per cent. However, this rate falls to 47 per cent for a person with 'moderate' disabilities, and to 25 per cent for a person with 'severe' disabilities. Globally, no overall figures seem to be available, although, the WHO (2007c) estimates that there are 470 million people of working age, and that for people with disabilities, unemployment rates are disproportionately high, with working conditions likely to be worse. The theme for the 2007 International Day of Persons with Disabilities was a call for 'decent work' (WHO, 2007c).

CASE STUDY

Helena's story

Helena has a learning disability and attended a mainstream primary school which she enjoyed. When she was 11 years old, she and her parents were told by the head teacher that she would not go to the local secondary school, but instead was going to be sent to a special school because she was "slow' at reading and writing. While she enjoyed the primary school experience, attending the special school led to her feeling worthless, and she learned to read and write with the help of her sister. At 15 years old she started helping – unpaid – in the special school's nursery department, but when she left school at 18 years old she was told that she would never secure a job. She went on to a training scheme which she found so boring that she left. A visit from a social worker was a turning point in Helena's life. She said that she was taken seriously and with the social worker's support gained a job as a part-time administrative assistant. After three years she moved to a full-time permanent post and now continues to hold a full-time salaried position.

(Adapted from Cree and Davis, 2006, pp109–114)

Helena's story shows how the potential of disabled people contrasts with their relatively poor educational opportunities – in her case severely limited by the policy decision of not providing a place in a mainstream secondary school. It also shows the potential of a positive attitude from a social worker – after all, it would have been relatively 'easy' for the social worker to try and persuade Helena to go back to the training scheme in the absence of any other provision. Most of all, however, it demonstrates Helena's very strong desire for work and self-determination. Her action of resistance (a theme we will explore later) and her social worker's support helped reverse the impact of poor policy decisions by other 'professionals'.

People with learning disabilities are more likely to be unemployed than other groups of disabled people. In the UK, for example, it is estimated that only 10 per cent of learning disabled people have any contact with the paid labour market (Turning Point, 2004). Price and Simpson (2007, p57) argue that while the integration of learning disabled people into communities has improved, exclusion from employment has increased mainly due to the development of a 'skill-based' economy. Those in jobs are invariably in low-paid employment. For all disabled people the question of access to both public spaces and transport (Oliver, 1990) creates more 'disabling barriers'. Price and Simpson (2007) point out that the key to social inclusion for disabled people is well-paid employment, which brings with it financial independence as well as feelings of self-worth and self-esteem – as illustrated by Helena's story.

Learning disabled people and the training centre

In 2007, Vicky Price visited training centres in three EU countries and here is a brief summary of her findings.

In Parma, Italy, there is a city scheme run by the Co-operative movement which seeks to provide training and employment for people with learning disabilities. The scheme runs for 12 learning disabled people at a time and they are all employed in various activities – for example making leather goods, which are then sold through various trade outlets. The aim is to develop workplace skills, leading to paid employment. There is a very high staff to disabled person ratio (at times one-to-one). There are close links with local employers, which have led to part-time work, based on what the individual participant can manage.

In Amsterdam, a training centre is being developed to train learning disabled people to build furniture for a retail supplier. There is a high staff to disabled person ratio, with emphasis upon developing skills and engaging in productive work. The levels of participants' benefit payments are enhanced by this employment, but there are fewer links to employers offering paid work.

In the UK some larger-scale training centres exist with lower staff to disabled person ratios and few links to employers offering paid work. There is a strong emphasis on work experience placements, some of which have resulted in learning disabled people spending six hours in 'work experience' for no pay, in order to avoid their benefit payments being affected.

(Price, 2008)

These scenarios reflect international trends. Disabled people are often excluded from paid employment and find 'work' mainly on training schemes. The format of these varies and a main difference is the level of training (seen through staff to disabled person ratios) and available links to the labour market.

Poverty

Poor educational opportunities, often leading to low or no job opportunities, combine to leave disabled people in poverty. A recent report for the Joseph Rowntree Trust suggested that it was the lack of suitable educational qualifications which had a significant impact on the ability to find work (Palmer, 2007). Although the Disability Rights Movement in the UK has had some success in ensuring greater employment rights for disabled people (Beresford and Croft, 2004), Palmer's report shows that in every category or qualification, disabled people are more likely to be without work than non-disabled people, suggesting that discrimination remains a significant factor. The report also found that half of disabled adults (one million people) in workless households are living in poverty, with social security benefits insufficient to lift them above the poverty threshold.

Belonging to a minority ethnic group adds to the likelihood of being unemployed for disabled people in the UK (Sefton, et al., 2006). This reflects the global trend, discussed in Chapter 2, for migrant groups around the world to be more likely to be in low-paid employment or out of work. In a study of refugees and asylum seekers with disabilities in the UK, Roberts and Harris (2002) found that key problems for many were isolation, difficulties with access to welfare benefits and care (due to legal, language and awareness barriers), unsuitable housing, and unmet aspirations for employment.

The experience of poverty is often lifelong. Families with a disabled child are more likely to experience poverty than other families. A report from a UK-based NGO showed that:

- one in six disabled children lives in a household struggling to afford food and heating;
- almost half of families have borrowed money from friends and family, with one in five using the cash to pay their heating bills;
- one in 14 children with a disability or medical condition is living under the threat of losing their home.

(Contact a Family, 2008)

Worldwide there are similar trends. James Wolfensohn, the former president of the World Bank, said in 2002:

> *Disabled people are [...] more likely than other people to live in grinding*
> *poverty. More than 1.3 billion people worldwide struggle to exist on less than*
> *[US]$1 a day, and the disabled in their countries live at the bottom of the pile.*

(Disability Knowledge and Research Programme, 2008)

The Disability Knowledge and Research (Disability KaR, 2008) programme, which has strong links with disabled people's groups worldwide, has shown that there is a need to develop disability projects as part of mainstream activities in the developing South. A key feature of their programmes is that disabled people themselves are included in the running of international development projects to help promote their social status. Among the 50,000 people who die each day as a result of extreme poverty, 10,000 are disabled (Yeo, 2005). In addition to experiencing poverty more intensely, disabled people are also found to have fewer opportunities to escape poverty than non-disabled people, for example because physical impairments make it difficult to work in the agricultural sector – which tends to be dominant in developing countries (Disability KaR, 2008).

CASE STUDY

Experiences of poverty in Rwanda
Claude

Claude has mobility difficulties after contracting polio when he was eight. He was the only person in his family to survive the genocide. He is married with four children under eight years old. He received housing from an NGO assisting victims of the genocide, but his home is 10km away from the one hectare of land he inherited from his parents. His mobility problems mean that it is difficult for him to cultivate it. His wife helps but it is hard with a young family. If he has money he hires a worker, but he is not getting full benefit from his land. He has thought about selling it, but land closer to his house is more expensive, so he could not afford to buy a hectare. He has thought about using his land as collateral for a loan, but he is not sure. He has tried to join local micro-credit initiatives but he has not always been able to keep up the weekly repayments.

Marie

Marie is 41 years old with two children. Marie had polio as a child that affected both legs. Her appliances are old and broken and she cannot afford to get them repaired. Her mobility difficulties prevent her from cultivating her small garden. She relies on her children to collect water 4km away otherwise she has to pay someone to collect it for her. Her household was the only one not to receive a goat through a European Commission development programme. She was told by the community leader that as she had no land and was disabled, she could not care for the goat. She cannot access micro-credit as she has no collateral and is considered a bad risk. Yet Marie is well educated. Simple repairs to her appliances would liberate her and enable her to lead an independent life again.

(Adapted from Thomas, 2005, p7)

It becomes clear that while poverty and disability are intertwined both in the developed North and in the developing South, the consequences of this relationship are more severe in developing countries.

Housing

There is a growing trend for integrated housing and for accessible buildings. Some countries in the global North have better records on this than others and despite building regulations, not all new buildings within the UK have good access for disabled people. The trend globally is moving away from institutional care towards developing integrated living schemes. Disabled people have been active in campaigns to bring about greater choice in their living arrangements, and have become very vocal opponents of institutional care. This global trend is linked to what is sometimes known as the 'globalisation of the personalisation agenda'.

RESEARCH SUMMARY

Kim (2008) – independent living in (South) Korea

In Korea, 'disability' is defined by strict criteria with six different categorisations. Ninety-eight per cent of disabled people live in the community, with 11 per cent unemployed (the unemployment rate for non-disabled people is 3 per cent), and with average monthly incomes 45 per cent lower compared to non-disabled people. The overall welfare budget for disabled people has increased, and Kim argues that this is related to the growing strength of the Disability Rights Movement, which has developed from being led by professionals and parents (with an emphasis on 'care') to being led by disabled people themselves (with an emphasis on 'rights'). This led to higher levels of choice, but there was also a realisation that severely disabled people were not benefiting from the new laws, leading to what Kim refers to as the current phase of 'diversification'. From 2001, Centres for Independent Living (CILs), influenced by policy development in Japan, were established across the country, albeit initially without financial support from the government. They are still primarily supported by funding from local government; private sources; fees for services and donations. CILs employ a high percentage of disabled people and aim to provide a range of services from advocacy and advice to independence skills training. Kim sets out some future challenges for the Disability Rights Movement.

- *Can it survive, given the relatively low levels of financial support provided for disabled people?*

- *How far can it apply to intellectually impaired people, bearing in mind that the main activists in the independent living movement are physically disabled?*

- *Should the movement develop to focus more on advocacy or on service provision?*

- *How far should the training aspect be extended? (CILs are led by disabled people, in contrast to other forms of independence training.)*

The conclusion is that the supporters of independent living programmes need to form global alliances, particularly when they live in countries where services are relatively underfunded.

Some of Kim's observations reinforce what we have already discussed concerning the impact of employment and poverty, as well as the role of disabled people themselves in programmes of advocacy. In some situations, however, independent living arrangements are questioned. In the Netherlands, residents of Dennendal, a group living arrangement developed in the 1970s, opposed government policy aimed at promoting independent living. Dennendal was seen as radical in its aim of creating a collective where learning disabled people lived, breaking with the traditions of medicalised models. As a result of the movement away from this group living model, the Dutch Government is proposing to withdraw funding from Dennendal and to ensure that residents are 'resettled' in integrated communities. Many of the residents do not want to leave (Rot, 2007). Another development in the Netherlands is that former large institutions are being redeveloped into smaller living units, built for disabled people, with non-disabled people building their homes in the surrounding grounds – a case of the community coming to disabled people, rather than the other way around (Vlaskamp and Poppes, 2004).

This raises questions about choice for disabled people, especially for learning disabled people. In the UK, while village communities are seen as one of the housing options promoted under current policy, in reality many local authorities do not fund such placements, as they instead actively seek to promote supported living. The debate is set to continue, but it does appear that choice is being denied, with a suspicion that the main focus is not on the well-being and wishes of learning disabled people, but on financial considerations.

Social work and disabled people: An international perspective

We have examined aspects of education, employment and training, poverty and housing for disabled people. An international perspective on social work would include all of these areas as 'social work', rather than using more rigid and restrictive definitions which are common in the UK. We have also shown how the movement away from large-scale institutions is global, and part of a developing rights-based approach. Internationally, there is also a strong emphasis on rehabilitation and health-based interventions, especially for people who have become disabled as a result of accidents or illness. In the developed North, it is easy to forget that globally the majority of disabled people lack access to health care of even the most basic kind. A key aim internationally is for rehabilitation to be community-oriented (WHO, 2006). The work of international organisations is based on the UN Convention for the Rights of Persons with Disabilities, which includes 50 separate articles. You should read the full text of the Convention, which can be accessed at: www.un.org/disabilities/default.asp?

One of the difficulties faced by disabled people in many developed countries is the number of different services they need to access and the range of different professionals who enter and leave their lives. The drive towards integrated services in the EU is intended to simplify this (Munday, 2007). Another feature is the need to ensure that disabled people are in charge of their own lives. This results in social workers and other professionals becoming resources for disabled people, rather than directing the management of their lives (Finkelstein, 1981).

Self-advocacy has a long history and is often linked to testimonies of resistance (Mitchell, et al., 2006), such as the stories of the American pioneers Ray Loomis and Tim Houlihan, who were members of the People First movement. Tim Houlihan travelled to Britain in the early 1980s and promoted self-advocacy. Given the history of social work with learning disabled people, it is not surprising that there are times when self-advocates are critical of professional social work interventions. Helena's story, earlier in this chapter, shows how social work support can be positive and help turn people's lives around.

It is also important that social workers do not lose sight of their responsibility to ensure the protection of vulnerable people. This should not be in conflict with the aims of self-advocacy movements, but acknowledge that there are times when some disabled people, for example those with learning disability, can experience bullying and more extreme forms of violence – sometimes resulting in death, as the case of Steven Hoskin in the UK showed (Morris, 2007).

What social workers do in any country is going to be determined by national and local policies for services. We have looked at services in a number of countries in this chapter and have seen how there are differences as well as similarities. We conclude by summarising a key publication in relation to learning disability and international perspectives.

RESEARCH SUMMARY

Adam's world chances

David Race is an academic who has spent over 30 years writing and researching aspects of learning or (to use his now preferred term) intellectual disability. The book summarised here is a comparison of seven countries and the services they have for learning disabled people. The countries are: Sweden; Norway; New Zealand; Australia; the USA; Canada; and the UK. They are all countries where English is widely spoken, and this may be a weakness in the book, but the interest lies in its approach. Race's adopted son, Adam, has Down's syndrome, and Race explores what it would be like for Adam to live in another country.

In all seven countries, there would be a lot of focus on service provision during Adam's early years, but the actual services received would differ. With the exception of Scandinavia, services provided would depend upon the parents' financial and social status, referring not just to their payment means, but to their ability to press for services which would promote inclusion.

Inclusive education without any parental pressure would be most likely to occur in Sweden and Norway. Outside Scandinavia, in the countries researched, the level of inclusive education would be more variable and depend more on parents' interventions. The country where mainstream inclusion was the least likely was the UK (even with parental pressure). The difference in other Anglophone countries is that there are more extensive parental organisations. In all countries with the exception of the UK, Adam's education would be work-related, and he would in many countries move on to sheltered occupations. In the UK, Adam would be most likely to go to college.

RESEARCH SUMMARY

Gaining paid employment would be difficult in all of the countries, but Adam would be more likely to gain meaningful daytime occupation in Sweden, Norway, New Zealand and Australia. Adam would be the most likely to choose with whom and where he could live in Sweden and Norway. In most of the countries, Adam would be living with his parents. In the UK, almost 65 per cent of learning disabled adults live with their parents, and almost a third have parents over the age of 65. Race's conclusion is that the countries where Adam would get the closest to living an 'ordinary life' would be Sweden and Norway.

(Race, 2007, pp221–4)

CHAPTER SUMMARY

In this chapter, we have considered how definitions and understandings of 'disability' differ internationally, and have examined the role of international debates and campaigns in this context. In particular, we have looked at the influence of the 'social model' of disability, and at the concept of 'normalisation' – which, despite their differences, have both played a significant role in shaping policies and services in many countries. We have also seen how the lives of disabled people around the world have been and continue to be affected by different approaches in the fields of education, employment/training, and housing – resulting in a variety of barriers as well as opportunities. The 'local' and the 'global' views reveal, overall, ongoing discrimination and exclusion of disabled people, as well as some positive examples of inclusion and self-determination. Both from a UK-based and from an international perspective, poverty continues to be a major problem for many disabled people. While in the global 'North', discrimination based on disability is often compounded by further disadvantages experienced by people from ethnic minorities, in countries of the 'South', the harshness of extreme poverty both as a cause and consequence of disability remains a common experience for many.

Despite the difficulties of widely differing resources worldwide, social work professionals (both in the UK and elsewhere) need to face the ongoing challenge of working in ways which open up opportunities for disabled people, promoting self-determination and inclusion, respecting self-advocacy and becoming a resource for disabled people – rather than trying to control or manage their lives.

FURTHER READING

Race, D (2007) *Intellectual disability: Social approaches*. Maidenhead: Open University Press.
This is an excellent book which sets out key elements of services for people with an intellectual disability in seven countries. Its unique strength is that it uses the case study of David Race's own adopted son and examines how he would have fared in each country.

Mitchell, D, Traustadottir, R, Chapman, R, Townson, L, Ingham N and Ledger, S (2006) *Exploring experiences of advocacy by people with learning disabilities: Testimonies of resistance*. London: Jessica Kingsley Press.
The book gives plenty of examples of how people with learning disabilities have engaged in various form of self-advocacy since the 1950s, and includes material from the USA, Canada, Australia, Iceland and the UK.

Chapter 8

Social work as an international profession: Origins, organisations and networks

Karen Lyons and Sue Lawrence

ACHIEVING A SOCIAL WORK DEGREE

This chapter will help you to meet the following National Occupational Standards for Social Work.
Key Role 6: Demonstrate professional competence in social work practice.
Unit 18 Research, analyse, evaluate, and use current knowledge of best social work practice.
19.3 Work within the principles and values underpinning social work practice.
Unit 20 Manage complex ethical issues, dilemmas and conflicts.

It will also introduce you to the following academic standards set out in the social work subject benchmark statement.
5.1.2 The service delivery context.
- the location of contemporary social work within historical, comparative and global perspectives, including European and international contexts.
5.1.3 Values and ethics.
- aspects of philosophical ethics relevant to the understanding and resolution of value dilemmas and conflicts in both interpersonal and professional contexts.
5.1.4 Social work theory.
- the relevance of sociological perspectives to understanding societal and structural influences on human behaviour at individual, group and community levels;
- the relevance of psychological, physical and physiological perspectives to understanding personal and social development and functioning.
5.1.5 The nature of social work practice.
- the place of theoretical perspectives and evidence from international research in assessment and decision-making processes in social work practice;
- the integration of theoretical perspectives and evidence from international research into the design and implementation of effective social work intervention, with a wide range of service users, carers and others.

Introduction

This chapter describes the international dimensions of the origins of social work and some of the organisations associated with its development in the late nineteenth and early twentieth centuries. We also introduce some of the social work associations which represent social work internationally today and consider some current examples of international networks and mobility of social workers (whether as educators, students or practitioners). Finally, we make some concluding comments in relation to this book as a whole and the need to develop international perspectives in social work.

An international history

From the beginning, there were examples of communication internationally between people who were establishing different forms of social work and of service developments which were springing up in different countries. In the latter part of the nineteenth century social work was developing in the UK and other European countries along several parallel paths but virtually all were related to the dire conditions of 'the urban poor'. There is no doubt that urbanisation was an important spur to the development of social work in most 'Northern' countries then, as it is in many parts of the recently industrialised or developing world now. In many cases the concentration of people in towns and cities reflected the migration of people from rural to urban areas seeking work. However, the rapid increase in the size of some cities also reflected international migration patterns, for instance the exodus of Irish people to (mainly) the USA following the famines of the 1840s or of Jewish people from central European countries later in the nineteenth (and again in the early and mid twentieth) century, in the face of persecution.

State provision for people who were destitute had been established in the UK through the workhouse system based on the 1834 Poor Law (sometimes called the New Poor Law, to distinguish it from the 1601 Poor Relief Act) although the provision of outdoor relief (financial assistance to people in their own homes) persisted in some areas of the country. Division of adults into those who could work and those who were unable to work because they were too sick in mind or body or too infirm also gave rise to the establishment of the asylums (and subsequently the work of Mental Health Officers, later to become Approved Social Workers) and to the provision of residential care for old people. The latter offered an alternative to those who were ineligible for the limited resources of the long-established almshouses where residence was often associated with membership of particular guilds or occupational groups. Similar developments were also evident in some European countries, such as Germany, though in many countries less systematised provision related to religious and charitable initiatives remained the norm. The 1834 Poor Law remained the basis for various welfare provisions in the UK for over 100 years, until it was 'replaced' by the 1948 National Assistance Act. This was the basis for local authority welfare departments which provided services for a range of vulnerable adults. This department was merged with children's departments to form social service departments following the Local Authority Social Services Act of 1970. In the first decade of the twenty-first century, responsibilities in relation to both children and adults under the overall control of the Department of Health were replaced by new arrangements which once again split social work services to children and families from those for adults at both central and local authority levels.

But it was another strand, outside state control, and related to the 'regulation' of charitable giving, that is credited by many as the forerunner of social work. The Charity Organisation Society (COS) was first established in England (1869) and used a system of voluntary workers to visit families receiving financial assistance from various charities to ensure that money received was 'spent wisely'. Records were kept of the different 'cases' and by the late nineteenth century training sessions had been set up for the volunteers. (These formed the basis of the first education and training courses for social workers in the UK in the early twentieth century, for example, at the London School of Economics and Birmingham University.) Similar schemes to COS were later established elsewhere, including in the USA (Buffalo in 1877) and the Caribbean (Kingston in 1900). The development of a form of 'casework' (which became a model for subsequent training and methods of intervention) was later heavily influenced by the 'psychiatric deluge' which followed developments in psychiatry and psychology in the 1920s and 1930s (Payne, 2005; Healy, 2001). COS itself changed its name and its focus in the second half of the twentieth century: it continued its work in the UK as the Family Welfare Association until 2008 and is now known as Family Action. (See website address in the resources section on page 125.)

Another major form of social work developed from the settlement houses. These were established (with funding from major universities and philanthropists) in poverty-stricken areas of major cities such as London, Birmingham, Liverpool and Glasgow, partly to offer residential accommodation but also to provide services for local populations, particularly women, children and young people. The residents spent part of their time as volunteers and their activities (including mother and toddler groups and after-school clubs) laid the basis for approaches later formalised in training for group and community work. The development of the first similar project in the USA (Hull House in Chicago in 1889) was attributed to the visit by an American pioneer of social work, Jane Addams, in the mid 1880s to Toynbee Hall (established in 1884) in London's East End. (See website addresses for Hull House and Toynbee Hall in the resources section on page 125.) Jane Addams also visited similar establishments in Germany and Hull House became a centre for services to address the needs of Irish and other immigrants (Kendall, 2000). Addams later worked with a German social worker, Alice Salomon (and others), to initiate international developments in the establishment of social work associations (Healy, 2001 and see later). It was in settlements in South and East London in the 1920s that Eileen Younghusband, an important figure in the mid-twentieth-century development of social work education in the UK and internationally, gained her early experience (Lyons, 2003) and many students on social work courses have gained practice experience in them up to the present. Most have long since lost their residential role and now operate rather as resource centres for local community groups.

However, other strands in the development of social work internationally were also evident in the establishment of organisations providing protection and care for children, and some of the agencies described by Heywood in her history of the development of child care services still play an important role in service provision today (Heywood, 1978). In some cases such organisations started as local and national initiatives which were then 'exported' so that branches or similar agencies were established in other countries. One such example is the National Society for the Prevention of Cruelty to Children (NSPCC, first established in London in 1884), which became a model for the foundation of Societies in countries such as Canada and Australia. In other cases the work of such organisations itself took on an international dimension. Mention has previously been made of the role of various child care agencies in the UK (including Barnado's and some of the denominational societies) in transporting children who were deemed to be 'orphans' to foster or adoptive homes in other countries (notably Australia and Canada). Although this practice formally ceased in the mid twentieth century (as late as the 1960s) it still has resonance as we hear of a French charity apparently seeking to 'export' children from Africa to France for adoption in 2007. These children were allegedly orphans from the Darfur region of Sudan, but were subsequently found to be children from Chad whose parents were still alive (*The Guardian*, 2007).

Other organisations grew from the plight of children caught up in international conflict. Save the Children is an international non-governmental organisation (INGO) which had its origins in work related to the 'rescue' and care of children who were destitute following the devastation in the Balkan Region resulting from the First World War (1914–18). An Englishwoman, Eglantyne Jebb, was the moving force in establishing this organisation, a primary function of which, initially, was fund-raising. However, Jebb was also a leading figure in drafting a Declaration of the Rights of the Child (in 1923) and getting this adopted by the League of Nations (the forerunner of the United Nations) (Healy, 2001). This declaration could be regarded as the first draft of an internationally accepted statement which was finally formalised as the UN Convention on the Rights of the Child (1989). The organisation itself has also continued with important work internationally, related to the effects of war, including running projects to rehabilitate child soldiers (in some African countries) and to care for unaccompanied refugee children and young people in the UK.

Other organisations have been established and continue to operate more specifically in the field of local and international poverty and disaster relief. Notable among these is the Red Cross (first established in the UK in 1863). This now has 'branches' around the world, including in some Muslim countries where it is known as the Red Crescent. Importantly, it provides services to people of all faiths and none, as can be seen in its work with refugees and asylum seekers in Greece (Lyons and Stathopoulos, 2001) but it is perhaps best known for providing help internationally in response to disasters. There are other organisations which have their roots and now their main branches more specifically in religious organisations and countries where a particular faith or denomination predominates. One such is CARITAS, which provides social services in many predominantly Catholic countries, including Spain and in Latin America, although it also provides services to people who are not members of the Roman Catholic Church.

Finally, in this brief (and far from comprehensive) summary of the international origins of social work and associated agencies, we should mention one more organisation, International Social Services (ISS). This was established in 1924 in Geneva and grew out of work with refugees by the Young Women's Christian Association (YWCA). ISS still has its head office in Geneva and social workers operate from here and a small number of national offices located in different countries, including the UK and Australia (Lyons,

1999). As indicated in the case studies in Chapters 3 and 6, this agency continues to offer services to individuals and families who have been adversely affected by migration. Staff based in national offices contact local social work agencies abroad, for example, to explore options for vulnerable people who might want to return to their countries of origin, or the advisability of overseas placement of children.

ACTIVITY 8.1

Browse the internet for one national and one international organisation given above to check how much information you already know. Make a note of any useful information new to you.

Comment

Although you may be familiar with some aspects of your chosen organisations, you will no doubt have found quite a lot of information that is new to you. It is important regularly to update your knowledge of both national and international organisations relevant to social work, by researching available information on the internet, in journals and in books.

International social work associations

Apart from the agencies which were established to offer social work services to individuals and communities, social workers also saw the need for the establishment of international membership associations to represent and promote the profession itself and to give it a voice at international level on behalf of people who are otherwise excluded from forums for debate and policy formation. To some extent these organisations had their origins in the networks formed by people, particularly women, who were active in various social movements in the early twentieth century, including those associated with votes for women and pacifism (Lorenz, 1994). Healy (2001) has described how some of the pioneers of social work (including Jane Addams and Alice Salomon) had the opportunity to meet at the International Congress of Women in Germany (in 1904), and the Congress of the International Council of Women in Canada (in 1909), and they became founders of the Women's International League for Peace and Freedom.

Healy goes on to describe (pp48–51) how the idea for an international conference specifically concerned with social work originated from European and Japanese social workers attending the National Conference of Social Work held in the USA in 1919. After various communications and with support from the American Association and the League of Red Cross Societies, an organising committee met in Paris in 1926 under the leadership of a Belgian (Dr René Sand) and began working collaboratively with other organisations to plan for an International Social Welfare Fortnight to be held in Paris in 1928. Thus, the 1928 International Conference of Social Work was, in fact, one of a series of Congresses led by different organisations and focusing on different social concerns. Nearly 2,500 people from 42 countries attended the Social Work Conference and one section of the proceedings was devoted to social work education (led by Alice Salomon). This gave rise to the establishment of the International Committee (later renamed Association) of Schools of Social Work (IASSW), representing, as its name suggests, schools of social work around the globe. IASSW can be seen as an offshoot of the International Conference of Social Work (ICSW), which subsequently became the International Council on Social Welfare, with membership drawn from a wide range of voluntary agencies active in the social welfare field.

These two associations have had a chequered but unbroken history since that time and have been important in promoting the international development and exchange of knowledge through organising periodic conferences and establishing (in the late 1950s) the first international journal concerned with social work and welfare developments, appropriately called *International Social Work* (*ISW*). However, it took rather longer to establish a third association, as an international representative of national associations of social workers, the International Federation of Social Workers (IFSW). This was finally established in 1956, at a Conference in Munich, following the demise of an earlier body, the International Permanent Secretariat of Social Workers. The headquarters of this organisation had been moved from Berlin to Prague due to the rise of Nazism in the late 1930s but in 1948 the political situation in Czechoslovakia made it impossible to operate (Dodds and Johannesen, 2006). The Federation soon joined ICSW and IASSW in joint ownership and editorial work of the journal and from the mid 1960s took responsibility for organisation of its own international conferences. However, a joint committee is meeting at the time of writing to plan a joint World Congress of all three organisations in Hong Kong in 2010.

We have already mentioned that an important role of all three organisations is the promotion of international exchange of knowledge: as in any professional field, this is partly done through research and the publication of journal articles. *International Social Work* celebrated its 50th year of publication in 2007 and continues to provide an important source of historic and contemporary material about social work in different countries and about comparative studies and international issues (not least since the digitalisation of back files and the placing of all material on the web) (Healy and Thomas, 2007). More recently, IASSW or IFSW have supported the establishment or maintenance of regional journals (in the Caribbean and Asia Pacific region respectively) and both organisations have programmes for publication of books on international themes and with contributions from authors in different parts of the world.

In addition to supporting the journal *ISW*, ICSW produces a regular series of Newsletters including contents which alert its members to international policy changes and new initiatives, for example, by the UN or its associated bodies. This relates to a second area of work which all three associations have carried out over the years with varying degrees of success. This is the area of advocacy work on behalf of social workers everywhere for the extension of human rights and social justice in all societies and in international economic and policy development. It can be noted here that IFSW established consultative status with the UN in 1959, a position changed to representative status with the United Nations Economic and Social Council in 1964. Since that time representatives of IFSW have engaged with personnel and different UN agencies to contribute to debates about new initiatives and policy developments, as described in a recent chapter by Cronin *et al*. (2006). However, as also identified in the IFSW book edited by Hall (2006) the role of advocacy and change agent, whether locally, nationally or internationally, does not sit comfortably with the roles of social workers and the functions ascribed to (or assumed by) their employing organisations in many countries and this can raise ethical dilemmas for social workers. One important and concrete activity of IFSW was the establishment in 1988 of its own Human Rights Commission to advocate for people undertaking social work whose human rights have been violated by their own governments (Lyons, 1999).

ACTIVITY 8.2

Open the web pages for ISFW, ICSW and IASSW and go to the Partnerships, UN or links section, respectively. Open up links for organisations with which you are not familiar. Make notes of websites with information relevant to social work.

Comment

You may have been surprised at how influential international organisations representing social work have become and may want to become a member. Membership of IFSW and ICSW is through a professional association of social workers; for example, in the UK the member association of IFSW is the British Association of Social Workers (BASW) although there are also opportunities for individuals to become 'Friends' of the Federation. Membership of ICSW is through umbrella organisations for voluntary associations so, for instance, IFSW or the IASSW are members. The latter, IASSW, is open to universities or colleges providing social work training but also has a membership section for individual educators.

This brings us to the third aspect of the work of these international organisations, which is to identify areas of commonality and difference between social work policies and practices in different parts of the world and to develop policy statement and ethical frameworks which can serve as guides to social work development in any country. IFSW has in the past produced policy documents on a range of topics including, for instance, globalisation and the environment (which, at the time of writing, is receiving the most hits on the website); HIV/AIDS; migration; and older persons. More recently, and as mentioned previously, the Association and the Federation have collaborated to produce the international definition of social work; a statement about ethics in social work; and a document about global standards in social work education. These were all produced in a supplement circulated with *ISW*, 50(1) in 2007 or are available on the websites of both organisations.

There are ongoing debates about the extent to which such international statements can have universal relevance, as was debated, for instance, in a special issue of the journal *Social Work Education*, 23(5), devoted to this topic in 2004. Similar concerns are sometimes voiced about UN Conventions, for instance, on Human Rights or on the Rights of the Child. Are there indeed some fundamental similarities in the needs of human beings of all races and nationalities or do such declarations, definitions and statements perpetuate 'Western' or 'Northern' colonisation or replicate, in an intellectual form, the domination of affluent countries in the global economy? It is true that social work associations, schools of social work and voluntary agencies from more affluent countries predominate in the respective membership of the three organisations – and that people who are English-speaking are also likely to be at an advantage (at least if seeking participation in the running of the associations) but there are also attempts to address such inequalities through differential subscription rates (for membership and conference attendance); language and translation policies; and projects in which National Associations or Councils from an affluent country are 'twinned' with ones from the South.

In relation to membership, in the case of IFSW this has grown from the 12 founding national associations (including Australia, Canada and the USA as well as nine European countries) in 1956 to over 80 by 2008, representing over 500,000 social workers in countries as diverse as Papua New Guinea, Iceland, South Korea and Brazil. Similarly, IASSW apparently shifted from being largely a 'European/ North American organisation' up to the 1960s (Eileen Younghusband took over the Presidency in 1961) to a body representing schools of social work around the world. This partly reflected the growth of social work education in Africa in the 1960s and 1970s and more recently in many Asian countries. The most recent expansion of membership has taken place among schools of social work newly or re-established in Central and Eastern Europe (since 1989) and in China (where there are now over 200 schools of social work, established since the mid 1990s). The wider membership of these international organisations is partly echoed in the recent extension from French and Spanish abstract translations in *International Social Work* to Arabic, Chinese and Russian.

Finally, we should note that ICSW, IFSW and IASSW also have different forms of regional groupings: these promote regional activities which are seen as more 'specific' to the concerns of a particular continent or smaller region. Among these, and of most direct relevance to British readers, are the European regions of the ICSW and IFSW and IASSW (the European Association of Schools of Social Work – EASSW). These arrange regional conferences in alternate years (sometimes jointly) and promote specific activities aimed at identifying, monitoring and influencing regional social welfare policies. For instance, the European region of IFSW recently ran a project to identify positive social work responses to social exclusion as it is experienced in different countries of the EU. However, it is not only through the activities of these well-established, formal organisations that current social workers, educators and students can participate in international activities and in the next section we consider some of the examples of ways in which social work continues to be an international profession, albeit sometimes at a regional rather than global level.

Some examples of international networks and mobility in social work

The expansion of education and training programmes for social work internationally and the existence of regional or bilateral programmes of financial support for university staff and students on a range of courses (including but not specific to social work) have assisted social workers to engage in international activities. However, this has particularly been the case at regional level for people studying in the countries of the European Union, where (since 1986) there has been a system of funding for exchange of students and staff, curriculum development and, more recently, research, through the ERASMUS, SOCRATES and other EU schemes. Social work staff and students have taken advantage of these schemes so that new networks have been formed and new initiatives developed outside the formal structures of the three organisations described above. In addition, employment conditions in many European countries and in some Commonwealth countries are different from the UK – in so far as the UK has a shortage of qualified social workers – and for this and other reasons more social workers are seeking employment outside the country in which they qualified. We shall say a little more about each of these trends which, we suggest, are currently contributing to the renewed internationalisation of social work.

One of the earliest networks to be established with the aid of European funding was the European Centre for Community Education (ECCE) in 1986, co-ordinated from Koblenz. This grew out of bilateral exchange programmes already initiated by the German staff and eventually extended to include schools of social work in over 20 countries, ranging from Greece to Sweden and from Ireland to the Czech Republic. This network undertook a range of activities which involved students of social work, social policy and youth and community work in intensive seminars: these involved students from two or three countries and focused on a range of topics, including migration. Some students also undertook practice placements abroad and, depending on the amount and variety of European elements in their programme, some students gained 'European' certification in addition to their national qualifications. Additionally, staff members from the participating universities held annual meetings to plan and review activities and in 1996 ECCE co-ordinated a successful bid to the European Commission to undertake research into the impact of the ERASMUS scheme in the area of the social professions, the results of which were disseminated (along with other activities) at a major conference in Germany in 1996 (Seibel and Lorenz, 1998).

This was the first of several such European conferences and one of the offshoots was the formation of a network – The International Social Work and Society Academy (TISSA – see resources section on page 125 for website address) and new conferences (since 2000) for students and staff concerned with doctoral research. This PhD network was also partly an offshoot of another network established under French leadership in the late 1990s to look at the development of doctoral studies in European countries. One of the findings of this project was the extent to which this can be a valuable form of 'knowledge creation' in social work (and related occupational groups such as social pedagogy in other European countries) but one which is not well developed – or only just gaining in importance in some countries. However, people who teach on social work courses (including in the UK) are increasingly expected to have PhD qualifications and to be active in research as well as teaching (Lyons and Lawrence, 2006).

The question of European qualifications in addition to national ones was also very much the focus of a course which has now been running since 1994 in Maastricht (Netherlands), an MA in Comparative European Social Studies (giving rise to the acronym, MACESS – see page 125 for website address). This course is in fact validated by the London Metropolitan University (so successful students are awarded a British degree) but provides an interesting example of collaborative work by staff from a number of countries across Europe who teach on the course or supervise students at the dissertation stage. The annual intake of about 20 students each year, also drawn from a range of countries and usually returning to varied occupational roles and agency positions, contributes to a growing European network of practitioners and managers, formally connected through the MACESS Alumni scheme (Lyons and Lawrence, 2006).

A more recently established but now very extensive network for schools of social work, the European Platform for Worldwide Social Work (EUSW – see page 125 for website address) was set up in 2001 with British, Italian and Swedish leadership with the goal of developing and disseminating the knowledge base on social work, service users, policy, practice, research and education. The network has established a number of working groups to meet its objectives, mainly concerned with gathering, comparing, developing and disseminating information. It also has a task force that is developing a virtual classroom in social work in Europe.

Another formal system of 'summer schools' for social workers (practitioners, academics and students) has been initiated by a network based in Croatia (Inter-University Centre Dubrovnik, IUC – see page 125 for website address) and this now provides opportunities for social workers to engage in symposia which focus on a particular topic for a week at a time. There are usually three such weeks in June each year. There are thus increasing opportunities at regional level for students and practitioners to access literature about social work in different countries and in the European context and to become involved in the activities of different networks, conferences or symposia.

ACTIVITY 8.3

Open the websites for IFSW, ICSW and IASSW and their regional offshoots (such as EASSW). Go to the conferences and publications sections. Identify events or publications you might like to explore further.

Comment

Some social workers are able to seek funding from their employer to facilitate attendance at regional events. Such activity is often considered Continuing Professional Development necessary for professional registration as a social worker. Subscription to journals such as *International Social Work* or the *European Journal of Social Work* helps to keep social workers in touch with innovations and developments in both national and international social work.

Some of this networking and dissemination activity, and indeed the drawing up of the *Global Standards* document by IASSW (2005) and IFSW, relates to a concern about comparability of national professional qualifications and the wish for these to be 'portable' and recognised in the case of social workers who wish to seek employment outside their country of qualification. Many countries, including the UK, have regulatory systems which require those wishing to practice in a particular country to register and it is to these bodies that 'foreign nationals' have to present evidence of their professional training and qualifications. Despite the cost and sometimes delays which such procedures might entail, we have seen an increase in the number of social workers from abroad seeking employment in the UK since about 2000. However, the ethical dimension of this movement, including the 'brain drain' that this might represent for some countries, has been recognised in the establishment of a (voluntary) *Social Care Code of Practice for International Recruitment* (posted on the website of the Social Care Institute for Excellence (SCIE, 2006) and also discussed in a recent article by Welbourne, et al. (2007)).

To some extent the increase in the number of social workers qualified abroad in the UK workforce was attributed to the demand for qualified social workers to take up posts in social service departments (particularly in relation to child protection work) and to the active recruitment of social workers from abroad. However, the supply of such social workers, particularly from countries such as South Africa and Zimbabwe, also reflects the lack of suitable posts or the deteriorating conditions for social workers in these countries. Therefore, jobs in the UK offer better opportunities professionally and personally for individuals and their families: social work was for a short time one of the occupations recognised by the Home Office as needing qualified staff and it was therefore able to recruit foreign nationals (who were then eligible for work permits and visas). However, there has since been more attention given to retention and local training initiatives as well as recruitment from within the European Union so the composition of the workforce is changing.

There are also other factors at work in the recruitment of overseas social workers. These include the wish by young social workers from countries such as Canada and Australia to visit Europe and sometimes to 'trace their roots' as well as gaining professional experience outside their own country. Additionally, some social workers have been recruited from countries such as India partly on the grounds of relevant ethnicity and/or language skills by departments in localities where there are high numbers of ethnic and linguistic minorities. Finally, there are increasing indications of the recruitment of staff from countries such as Germany and Spain, where full-time and/or permanent job opportunities for qualified social workers have been limited for some time; or from Romania where the relatively recent establishment and rapid expansion of social work education has not been matched by a similar expansion in the amount of paid work available in public or voluntary social service agencies (Lyons and Littlechild, 2006).

Apart from the still relatively small numbers of 'overseas staff' now practising as social workers in the UK, we can also note the increase in the number of people from abroad working in the wider social care field, notably in the area of residential and domiciliary care for older people. Recent estimates suggest that of the one million people working in the social care sector (including social workers) 95,000 were born outside the UK; and that, of migrants from the most recent countries to join the European Union (specifically the eight from the former communist bloc, including Poland), 3 per cent work in the social care sector (Philpott, 2007). While recruitment to the elder care residential services has traditionally been from countries such as the Philippines (enabling women to gain employment in the UK and then send money home to their families), there are indications that this sector will be increasingly dependent on labour from within the European Union, since rules governing the employment of overseas staff have changed and social care staff are not covered by the Home Office essential workers permits. This is an area where the personal and professional needs and aspirations of individuals may clash with national and European Union laws and policies in relation to both migration and employment.

Whatever the reason for the mobility of social workers and others in social services across national borders, we can note that, as well as posing challenges to the individuals concerned and to the agencies which employ them (and perhaps also sometimes to the user groups to which they relate) particularly in terms of cultural adaptation and sometimes language competence, increased mobility offers important opportunities to recognise the skills and experience which individual workers from other countries bring; and, at a more general level, increased opportunities for gaining an international perspective on the development of social work and social services.

C H A P T E R   S U M M A R Y

In this chapter we have reflected on the origins of social work in the UK in particular and on the way in which social work began to have an international dimension from its earliest stage of development. We have seen how particular individuals were instrumental in transferring ideas about practice and service developments from one country or continent to another (for example, Jane Addams) – or were the originators of conventions which became internationally accepted (for example, Eglantyne Jebb).

We have also identified the origins of particular agencies in the conditions of late-nineteenth and early-twentieth-century England and seen how similar conditions in other ('Northern') countries gave rise to the establishment of overseas branches or of autonomous agencies with similar titles and remits. We have also identified the ways in which the work of some of these organisations took on an international dimension or how their very establishment was a response to the particular conditions caused by international events. We noted in passing that the work of some of these agencies continues to this day, albeit in ways which reflect changes in need and conditions.

However, we can also note here that, in some respects, there has been very little change in the situations which we label as 'social problems' – not least those related to migration – or that, at the very least, we now see similar concerns presenting themselves in other societies which are at earlier stages of development in economic and sometimes political terms. Thus, while we in the UK and other European countries have moved to a recognition of poverty as a relative rather than an absolute concept, the experience of social exclusion is still very real for some minorities in 'affluent' societies – and the experience of poverty is still absolute in some of the countries from which some minority groups have emigrated.

We went on to introduce the three major international organisations formed to represent different constituencies of social work at the global level, IASSW, ICSW and IFSW; and to say something about the roles which they now perform. These member organisations have been important in identifying social work as a profession which is not restricted to a given time or place, although the exact form it takes will reflect both of these dimensions (as has been partially illustrated in some of the preceding chapters). The organisations have provided opportunities for exchange of ideas and information both within the profession and between social work and the wider social movements and organisations which affect us globally, not least the United Nations. Just as some of the pioneers of social work were involved in wider social movements, for example related to peace, so many social workers are now engaging (sometimes through the medium of these organisations) with current issues related to environmental conditions as well as with the more familiar themes of conflict resolution and migration.

Finally, we looked at some more recent and less formal examples of opportunities for social workers to engage in international debate and activities, including through participation in networks and education and training programmes. It has been suggested that the qualities needed of a good social worker are the ability to think, to act and to relate – and it is perhaps through relating to people of other cultures and countries that we learn most about what it means to have an international perspective and to utilise this perspective in our thinking and actions, whether at local, national, regional or international levels.

In conclusion

We have aimed in this book to introduce the idea of 'International Social Work'. While we suggest that some social workers may be involved in specialist forms of work at international levels, we are more concerned here with the need for *all* social workers to recognise the international dimensions of work at local level and to feel better prepared for the opportunities for transnational social work which, we suggest, are increasingly likely to arise in the normal course of daily practice. The increase in international migration; the speed of travel and communications; and the effects of a globalised economy mean that we are all interconnected in ways which are more significant in the twenty-first century than they have ever been. Old problems have taken on new forms and social workers are challenged to engage with international issues such as inter-country adoption; forced marriage; people-smuggling and trafficking; and increased drugs availability and usage.

Some of the skills and knowledge needed to practise from an international perspective perhaps mainly require a 'reframing' of existing knowledge and skills, but we have also suggested that in addition there are new areas of knowledge and skills needed to enhance practice which is sensitive to the impact of globalisation and the needs of particular user groups. Some of this new knowledge needs to be comparative. We have suggested that a profession which we can recognise as 'social work' exists in many countries across the world; that it has international roots; and that its shared value base constitutes an important aspect of its identity – but there are also significant variations in its local forms and functions.

As we have noted in the preceding chapters, most developed countries have services for a similar range of user groups although the organisation of such services varies, as do the qualifications and titles of the social workers themselves and the forms of intervention they favour. Extending our knowledge about the organisational settings and actual practices of social workers abroad can help us to reflect on our own practices and local services in ways which may result in useful developments. As also mentioned, in less developed countries, social professionals may be more involved in community development and nation-building activities; and may be more likely to work in conflict or 'post-disaster' situations. Social workers (including from the 'North') may be employed in international non-governmental organisations (such as the Red Cross/Red Crescent) and public social welfare provision may be limited. Finally, in this book we have included reference to international conventions and standards which can provide frameworks for assessing the efficacy of national legislation and policies as well as guidelines for new developments. Similarly, we have identified a range of organisations which have specialist roles and knowledge and/or which can afford opportunities for networking across international borders. In fact, substantial opportunities now exist (including conferences, publications and the web) for learning more about social work in other places and for identifying international resources which are relevant to social work developments at national and local levels.

Hall, N (ed) (2006) *Social work: Making a world of difference: Social work around the world IV*. Oslo: IFSW/FAFO.

This book was published to coincide with the 50th anniversary of the foundation of the International Federation of Social Workers. It provides readers with some information about the organisation itself and insight into its areas of concern and activity, not least by taking ethics in social work as a major theme in relation to many of its chapters. These include chapters on a range of relevant topics, such as child poverty, HIV/AIDS and migration, as well as others comparing ethical codes from different countries or perceptions of social work in Europe and the USA.

Web-based resources for international social work

International resources are listed under the following categories:

- international organisations and human rights conventions;

- sources for comparing countries' social policy and national statistics;

- resources about migration and asylum seekers, including the myths;

- sites about the European Union, its policies and opportunities for exchanges, study visits and projects;

- resources for working with particular service user groups;

- historical perspectives on international social work;

- examples of international social work education initiatives.

International organisations and human rights conventions

- United Nations (UN), **www.un.org/**

- World Health Organization (WHO), **www.who.int**

- The International Red Cross and Red Crescent Movement, **www.redcross.int/en/default.asp**

- Human Rights Watch, **www.hrw.org/**

- Amnesty International, **www.amnesty.org/**

- Oxfam, **www.oxfam.org/**

- Christian Aid, **www.christianaid.org.uk/**

- International Labour Organisation, **www.ilo.org/**

- United Nations Universal Declaration of Human Rights, **www.un.org/rights/**

- European Convention on Human Rights (ECHR) from the Council of Europe, **conventions.coe.int/Treaty/en/Treaties/Html/005.htm**

- United Nations Convention on the Rights of the Child, **www.unicef.org/crc/**

- The Geneva Conventions are discussed on the International Committee Red Cross site, **www.icrc.org/Web/Eng/siteeng0.nsf/htmlall/genevaconventions**

- Human rights in the UK explained on the Liberty website, **www.yourrights.org.uk/**

- The UK Equality and Human Rights Commission, **www.equalityhumanrights.com**, which since 2007 has taken over the functions of the Commission for Racial Equality (CRE), the Disability Rights Commission (DRC) and the Equal Opportunities Commission (EOC), as well as responsibilities for sexual orientation, age, religion and belief, and human rights.

International social work organisations

- International Association of Schools of Social Work, **www.iassw-aiets.org/**

- International Federation of Social Workers, **www.ifsw.org**

- European Association of Schools of Social Work, **www.eassw.org**

- International Council on Social Welfare, **www.icsw.org**

- International Social Services, **www.iss-ssi.org** (UK section: **www.issuk.org.uk**)

Comparative social policy and statistics

- Social security websites around the world and national offices, **www.ssa.gov/international/links.html**

- CIA website for global comparative data, **www.cia.gov/library/publications/the-world-factbook/**

Migration and asylum

- International Organisation for Migration, **www.iom.int/**

- United Nations High Commissioner for Refugees (UNHCR), an impartial humanitarian organisation mandated by the United Nations to lead and co-ordinate international action for the worldwide protection of refugees and the resolution of refugee problems, **www.unhcr.org.uk/**

- One World, **uk.oneworld.net/guides/refugees/**

- Refugee Council, **www.refugeecouncil.org.uk**

- Oxfam and myths about asylum seekers, **www.oxfamgb.org/ukpp/safe/mythsindex.htm**

- The Medical Foundation for the Care of Victims of Torture, **www.torturecare.org.uk**

- The UK Home Office Border Agency, **www.ukba.homeoffice.gov.uk/**

- BBC 'Born Abroad' websites: **http://news.bbc.co.uk/1/shared/spl/hi/uk/05/born_abroad/html/overview.stm**

The European Union

- Gateway to the European Union, **europa.eu/index_en.htm** and the *activities, institutions, documents and services* including the *European Union at a Glance*, **europa.eu/abc/index_en.htm**

- European Union statistical database, **epp.eurostat.ec.europa.eu/**

- Study abroad, **ec.europa.eu/education/programmes/llp/erasmus/students_en.html**

Service user groups

Children and young people

- The National Refugee Integration Forum, **www.nrif.org.uk/Education/index.asp**, which provides material to assist with all aspects of work with refugee children and their education – an essential resource.

- The National Association for Language Development in the Curriculum, **www.naldic.org.uk/.** While the focus of the website is language development for children whose first language is not English, it also contains very useful information about education for refugee and asylum-seeking children, as well as links to other websites.

- UNICEF UK, **www.unicef.org.uk/whatwedo/index.asp**, which contains much useful information about the position of children in the UK and also worldwide.

- UNICEF's 2007 campaign, 'Slave Britain', **www.unicef.org.uk/campaigns/slave_britain/index.html**

- The International Save the Children Alliance, **www.savethechildren.net/**

People experiencing mental ill health

- HM Government's Mental Health home page – up-to-date information about mental health policy in England, **www.dh.gov.uk/en/Healthcare/nationalServiceframeworks/Mentalhealth/index.htm**

- *Well Scotland*. The Scottish Government's programme for mental well-being. The website contains a section which gives personal stories, **www.wellscotland.info/index.html**

- MIND. Major UK campaigning mental health charity, **www.mind.org.uk/**

- *Mental Health in the EU* (European Union Public Health Information System), **www.euphix.org/object_class/euph_mental_health_eu.html**. An EU resource where you can gather material about the EU's policies to develop mental well-being.

- *Promoting the Mental Health Agenda,* **www.supportproject.eu/.** A European Union website which does what it says!

- *Sure Search,* **www.suresearch.org.uk/index.html.** A network of service users' research and education supported by the Centre of Excellence in Inter-disciplinary Mental Health, Birmingham University.

Disabled people

- Disabled People's International, **www.dpi.org/,** a network of national organisations or assemblies of disabled people, established to promote human rights of disabled people.

Historical perspectives

- The Child Migrants Trust, **www.childmigrantstrust.com**. Established in 1987 by a Nottingham social worker, this organisation provides support and information in relation to the forced migration of British children to overseas colonies until the 1970s.

- Family Action, an organisation supporting vulnerable families, was founded in the 1880s as the Charity Organisation Society (and, until 2008, was known as the Family Welfare Association), **www.family-action.org.uk/**

- Hull House, founded by the social work pioneer Jane Addams, **www.hullhouse.org**

- Toynbee Hall, founded in the mid 1880s as part of the Settlement movement, **www.toynbeehall.org.uk**

International social work education

- Master of Arts Comparative European Social Studies taught in Maastricht and London, **www.macess.nl/**

- Professional doctorate in International Social Work at London Metropolitan University, **www.londonmet.ac.uk/research/the-graduate-school/research-degrees/international**

- The International Social Work and Society Academy, **www.tissa.net**

- The European Platform for Worldwide Social Work, **www.eusw.net**

- The Inter-University Centre Dubrovnik, IUC, **www.iuc.hr/**

Glossary

Capacity building   activities which strengthen the knowledge, abilities and skills of individuals, organisations, communities or societies, with the aims of increasing or achieving empowerment, self-reliance, equity and sustainability.

Demographics (Demography)   information about the characteristics of a population, such as age, gender, race, income, educational attainment or location. *Demography* is the statistical study of populations.

Diaspora   the mass migration or 'dispersion' (either forced or voluntary) of a group of people sharing the same ethnic identity, to a different (usually distant) geographic location.

Globalisation   although often referred to as a mainly economic process (i.e. the breakdown of borders and barriers to international trade), globalisation has many different definitions, and can be seen as a term describing a multitude of (economic, political, social, technological, cultural, etc.) transformations which lead to greater interconnectedness of people and systems across the world.

Human capital/social capital   both terms refer to the notion that people (and their relationships) can be important and valuable resources. Human capital usually refers to the knowledge, skills and experience of people in the context of their role in the labour force. Social capital, on the other hand, refers to the contacts between, and networks of, individuals and groups – which are important for many areas of life (including, sometimes, finding employment).

Human rights   the basic rights and freedoms to which all people are entitled. A distinction is often made between civil and political rights on the one hand, and social, economic and cultural rights on the other (as well as between individual and communal rights). Human rights are generally considered as universal, inalienable, and indivisible.

International Association of Schools of Social Work (IASSW)   the international association of higher education schools, organisations and individuals involved in providing social work education. Its European branch, the *European Association of Schools of Social Work* (EASSW) includes about 300 different schools, universities and institutions supporting social work education.

International Council on Social Welfare (ICSW)   a global network of civil society organisations promoting social welfare, social development and social justice. It was founded in Paris in 1928 as the 'International Conference of Social Work', and changed its name to ICSW in 1967.

International Federation of Social Workers (IFSW)   an international network of national organisations representing social workers. Established in 1956, IFSW succeeded the *International Permanent Secretariat of Social Workers*, which was founded in Paris in 1928.

Migration (immigration, emigration)   the movement of people, either within a country (internal migration), or across international boundaries (international migration). Emigration refers to people leaving a country, to settle in another – immigration describes the same process from the perspective of the country of settlement.

Refugee   defined under the UN Convention relating to the Status of Refugees (1951) as a person who has left their country and is unable to return because of 'a well-founded fear of being persecuted for reasons of race, religion, nationality, membership of a particular social group or political opinion'. A person seeking asylum is applying to be recognised as having such a well-founded fear, and to be protected under international law as a result.

Remittances   money sent by labour migrants to their families in their countries of origin. Worldwide, remittances make a higher contribution to economic growth in developing countries than international aid.

Social justice   refers to justice which goes beyond the mere legal administrative system of a society, but which affords people fair treatment and a fair share of the benefits of a society.

Social pedagogy/social pedagogues   a concept and academic tradition in the wider field of social work, which originates, and is practised, in a number of European countries, including Germany and Scandinavia. Social pedagogy has a closer connection with education than is common within the traditions of UK social work, and is based on a holistic understanding of how individuals and communities develop and interact.

Social professionals   a term used to include different groups of professionals who practise social work in a wider sense (compared to a more 'narrow' definition of social workers in the UK). In an international context, this can include professionals working in fields such as community development or youth work.

Subsidiarity   an idea originally derived from the teachings of the Catholic Church, which is based on the principle that where the family, community or voluntary sector can provide social services, the state should intervene as little as possible in the delivery of such services (although state *funding* might still provide the basis of the services). The principle of subsidiarity has been, and continues to be, influential in the development and delivery of social services in a number of European countries.

Transnational (international, cross-national) social work   transnational social work usually refers to working across, or transcending, national boundaries. It is sometimes used interchangeably with the terms 'international' or 'cross-national' social work. However, unlike transnational or cross-national practice, social work can, as this book argues, have 'international' dimensions even where practitioners do not directly interact with anyone who is located in another country.

Virtual community   a community is a group of people who interact with each other, often organised according to shared values. While the traditional definition of 'community' included a shared geographical location, this is no longer the case, as members of *virtual communities* use media such as the internet to interact with each other.

References

Advisory, Conciliation and Arbitration Service (ACAS) (2005) *Religion or belief and the work place*. ACAS Publications. **www.acas.org.uk**

Age Concern España (2008) **www.acespana.org**

Anderson, KM (2007) Charting a course into the unknown: Banda Aceh, Indonesia, Tsunami, 2004. *Perspectives in Psychiatric Care*, 43(1): 47–51.

Arber, S (2006) Gender trajectories: How age and marital status influence patterns of gender inequality in later life. In Daatland, S and Biggs, S (eds) *Ageing and diversity*. Bristol: Policy Press.

Avramov, D and Maskova, M (2003) *Active ageing in Europe*. Strasbourg: Council of Europe.

Barker, P and Buchanan-Barker, P (2005) *The tidal model: A guide for mental health professionals.* Hove: Brunner-Routledge.

Barnes, C, Mercer, G and Shakespeare, T (1999) *Exploring disability: A sociological introduction*. Cambridge: Polity Press.

BBC News (2006a) People trafficking centre opens. 3 October 2006. **http://news.bbc.co.uk**

BBC News (2006b) Man guilty of 21 cockling deaths. 24 March 2006. **http://news.bbc.co.uk**

BBC News (2008a) Charities fear over failed banks. 10 October 2008. **http://news.bbc.co.uk**

BBC News (2008b) In full: Councils facing losses. 17 October 2008. **http://news.bbc.co.uk**

BBC News (2008c) Job fears over Iceland investment. 29 October 2008. **http://news.bbc.co.uk**

Bell, D (1980) The social framework of the information society. In Forester, T (ed) *The microelectronical revolution: The complete guide to the new technology and its impact on society*. Oxford: Blackwell Publishing.

Bennett, T, Savage, M, Silva, E, Warde, A, Modesco, G-C and Wright, D (2006) *The social organisation of media practices in contemporary Britain. A report for the British Film Institute.* **www.bfi.org.uk**

Beresford, P and Croft, S (2004) Service users and practitioners reunited: The key component for social work reform. *British Journal of Social Work*, 34(1): 53–68.

Berry, L (2006) A view from the General Social Care Council. In Lyons, K and Littlechild, B (eds) *International mobility of labour in social work*. Birmingham: Venture Press.

Beveridge, W (1942) *Social insurance and allied services*. London: HMSO.

Blakemore, K and Boneham, M (1994) *Age, race and ethnicity*. Buckingham: Open University Press.

Bolloten, B and Spafford, T (2005) *Refugee and asylum seeker children in UK schools*. National Association for Language Development in the Curriculum (NALDIC). **www.naldic.org.uk**

Bonnetti, L and Manfredi, F (2007) *Examples of good practice in elder care in the Parma municipality.* Paper given at EASSW Conference, Parma, Italy.

Bowker, J (2005) The rise and rise of the Scottish call centre. *The Scotsman Business*, 12 August 2005. **http://business.scotsman.com**

Brah, A (2001) Reframing Europe: Gendered racisms, ethnicities and nationalisms in contemporary Western Europe. In Fink, J, Lewis, G and Clarke, J (eds) *Rethinking European welfare*. London: Sage.

Bretherton, I (1992) Attachment and bonding. In Herson, M (ed) *Handbook of social development: A lifespan perspective*. New York: Plenum Press.

British Association of Social Workers (2002) *The code of ethics for social workers.* **www.basw.co.uk**

British Psychological Society (2009) *Western and African mental health*. **www.bps.org.uk**

Bunting, M (2005) Consumer capitalism is making us ill: We need a therapy state. *The Guardian*, 5 December 2007.

Burholt, V (2004) The settlement patterns and residential histories of older Gujaratis, Punjabis and Sylhetis in Birmingham, England. *Ageing and Society*, 24(3): 383–409.

Bytheway, B (1995) *Ageism*. Buckingham: Open University Press.

Calhoun, C (1998) Community without propinquity revisited: Communications technology and the transformation of the urban public sphere. *Sociological Inquiry*, 68(3): 373–97.

Campanini, A (2007) Social work in Italy. *European Journal of Social Work*, 10(1): 107–16.

Cannan, C, Lyons, K and Berry, L (1992) *Social work and Europe*. Basingstoke: Macmillan.

Carby, HV (1982) White woman listen: Black feminism and the boundaries of sisterhood. In Centre for Contemporary Cultural Studies, *The empire strikes back: Race and racism in 1970s Britain*. London: Hutchinson Education.

Carers UK (2007) Support for Black, Asian and minority ethnic carers: A good practice briefing. **www.carersuk.org**

Carey, M (2008) What difference does it make? Contrasting organisation and converging outcomes regarding the privatisation of state social work in England and Canada. *International Social Work*, 51(1): 83–94.

Casciani, D (2005) *Morecambe Bay: One year on.* BBC News, 5 February 2005. **http://news.bbc.co.uk**

Castells, M (2001) *The internet galaxy: Reflections on the internet, business and society*. Oxford: Oxford University Press.

Castles, S and Miller, MJ (1998) *The age of migration: International population movements in the modern world.* London: Macmillan.

Cemlyn, S and Briskman, L (2003) Asylum, children's rights and social work. *Child and Family Social Work,* 2003 (8): 163–78.

Centre du Rhône d'Information et d'Action Sociale en faveur des retraités et des personnes âgées (CRIAS) (2008) **www.crias.asso.fr**

Centre Pluridisciplinaire de Gérontologie (CPDG) (2008) **webu2.upmf-grenoble.fr**

Chand, A (2001) The overrepresentation of Black children in the child protection system: Possible causes, consequences and solutions. *Child and Family Social Work,* Vol. 5, 67–77.

Chevigny, B (2007) *Child soldiers demobilised in the Central African Republic.* UNICEF. **www.unicef.org**

CIA World Factbook (2009) **www.cia.gov**

Clarke, C L (2000) *Social work ethics: Politics, principles and practice.* London: Macmillan Press.

Cochrane, A and Clarke, J (1993) *Comparing welfare states: Britain in an international context.* London: Sage Publications in association with the Open University.

Cohen, S and Scull, A (eds) (1983) *Social control and the state.* Oxford: Blackwell.

Contact a Family (2008) *Counting the costs.* London: Contact a Family. **www.cafamily.org.uk**

Conway, J, Little, P, and McMillan, M (2002) Congruence or conflict? Challenges in implementing problem-based learning across nursing cultures. *International Journal of Nursing practice,* 8(5): 235–39.

Cooper, D (1968) *Psychiatry and anti-psychiatry.* London: Tavistock.

Cox, D and Pawar, M (2006) *International social work: Issues, strategies and programs.* London: Sage Publications.

Crawford, L and Walker, J (2003) *Social work and human development.* Exeter: Learning Matters.

Crawford, L and Walker, J (2008) *Social work with older people.* 2nd edition. Exeter: Learning Matters.

Crawley H. (2006) *Child first, migrant second: Ensuring that every child matters.* Immigration Law Practitioners Association (ILPA) Policy Paper. London: ILPA.

Cree, VE and Davis, A (2006) *Social work: Voices from the inside.* London: Routledge.

Cronin, M. Mama, RK, Mbugua, C and Mouravieff-Apostol, E (2006) Social work and the United Nations. In Hall, N (ed) *Social work: Making a world of difference: Social work around the world IV.* Oslo: IFSW/FAFO.

Curtis, P (2007) Record exodus leaves ageing Blighty. *The Guardian,* 23 August 2007. **www.guardian.co.uk**

Deegan, P (1996) Recovery as a journey of the heart. *Psychiatric Rehabilitation Journal,* 19(3): 91–97.

Department of Health (2001) *National service framework for older people.* **www.dh.gov.uk**

Department of Health (2004a) *The ten essential shared capabilities: A framework for the whole of the mental health workforce*. London: DH Publications. (Online version accessible at: **www.mhhe.heacademy.ac.uk**

Department of Health (2004b) *Religious and cultural awareness – a guide*. **www.info.doh.gov.uk**

Department of Health (2007) *Putting people first: A shared vision and commitment to the transformation of adult social care*. **www.dh.gov.uk**

Dingwall, R, Eekelaar, J and Murray, T (1995) *The protection of children: State intervention and family life*. Oxford: Basil Blackwell.

DirectGov (2008) *Definition of 'disability' under the Disability Discrimination Act (DDA)*. **direct.gov.uk**

Disability Discrimination Act, 1995. HM Government. London: The Stationery Office.

Disability Discrimination Act, 2005. HM Government. London: The Stationery Office.

Disability Knowledge and Research Programme (2008) *Lessons from the Disability Knowledge and Research Programme*. **www.disabilitykar.net**

Disability Rights Commission (DRC) (2005) *Disability Rights Commission submission to the Equality Review, 2005*. **www.equalityhumanrights.com**

Disability Rights Commission (2007) *Disability briefing May 2007*. **www.equalityhumanrights.com**

Disabled People's International (2005) *DPI Postition Paper on the Definition of Disability*. **v1.dpi.org**

Dodds, I and Johannesen, T (2006) Forward: Fifty years of IFSW. In Hall, N (ed) *Social work: Making a world of difference: Social work around the world IV*. Oslo: IFSW/FAFO.

Domicile collectif Nantes et communauté urbaine (2008) **www.nantesentourage-clic.nantes.fr**

Donnelly, M (1992) *The politics of mental health in Italy*. London: Tavistock/Routledge.

Dorling, D and Thomas, B (2004) *People and places: A 2001 census atlas of the UK*. Bristol: Policy Press.

Dosanjh, JS and Ghuman, PAS (1997) Punjabi child rearing in Britain: Development of identity, religion and bilingualism. *Childhood, a Global Journal of Child Research*, 1997 (4): 285–303.

Durkheim, E (2002) *Suicide*. London: Routledge (first published: 1887).

Elliot, L (2008) UN poised to play 'catch-up'. **www.guardian.co.uk**

Elliot, L and McCurry, J (2008) Biggest economies caught in 'storm of the century'. *The Guardian*, 31 October 2008. **www.guardian.co.uk**

Faragher, EB, Cass, M and Cooper, CL (2005) The relationship between job satisfaction and health: A meta-analysis. *Occupational and Environmental Medicine*, 62(2): 105–12.

Finkelstein, V (1981) Disability and the helper/helped relationship: A historical view. In Brechin, A, Liddiard, P and Swain, J (eds) (1981) *Handicap in a social world*. London: Hodder and Stoughton.

Foucault, M (1967) *Madness and civilisation*. New York: Pantheon Books.

Foucault, M (1977) *Discipline and punish*. Harmondsworth: Penguin.

Franklin, B (ed) (2002) *The new handbook of children's rights: Comparative policy and practice*. London: Routledge.

Fromm, E (2002) *The sane society*. London: Routledge Classics (originally published in 1955, New York: Holt, Rinehart and Winston).

Fryer, D (1995) Labour market disadvantage, deprivation and mental health. *The Psychologist*, 8(6): 265–72.

Gbla, O (2003) Conflict and post-war trauma among child soldiers in Liberia and Sierra Leone. In Sesay, A (ed) *Civil wars, child soldiers and post conflict peace building in West Africa*. Lagos: AFSTRAG.

General Social Care Council (2007) *Protection, professionalism, pride: Annual report 2005–2006*. **www.gscc.org.uk**

George, J (1997) Global graying: What role for social work? In Hokenstad, M and Midgley, J (eds) *Issues in international social work*. Washington, DC: NASW Press.

Geyer, R (2000) *Exploring European social policy*. Cambridge: Polity Press.

Gittens, D (1997) *The child in question*. London: Palgrave Macmillan.

Glyn, A. (2006) *Capitalism unleashed: Finance, globalisation and welfare*. Oxford: Oxford University Press.

Goffman, E (1961) *Asylums*. Harmondsworth: Penguin.

Government of Ireland (2006) *A vision for change: Report of the Expert Group on Mental Health Policy*. Dublin: Department of Health and Children/The Stationery Office. (Online version available at: **www.dohc.ie**

Graham, M (2002) *Social work and African-centred world views.* Birmingham: Venture Press.

Gray, M and Fook, J (2004) The quest for a universal social work: Some issues and implications. *Social Work Education*, 23(5): 625–44.

Hall, N (ed) (2006) *Social work: Making a world of difference: Social work around the world IV*. Oslo: IFSW/FAFO.

Harding, L (2006) German birth rate falls to lowest in Europe. *The Guardian*, 15 March 2006.

Hayes, D and Humphries, B (2004) *Social work, immigration and asylum*. London: Jessica Kingsley Publishers.

Health Care Commission (2005) *Count me in: Results of a national census of inpatients in mental health hospitals and facilities in England and Wales*. London: Commission for Health Care Audit and Inspection.

Healy L (2001) *International social work: Professional action in an interdependent world*. Oxford: Oxford University Press.

Healy, L and Thomas, R (2007) *International social work*: A retrospective in the 50th year. *International Social Work*, 50(5): 581–96.

Hetherington, R, Cooper, A, Smith, P, and Wilford, G (eds) (1997) *Protecting children: Messages from Europe*. Lyme Regis: Russell House Publishing.

Heywood, J (1978) *Children in care: The development of services for the deprived child*. 3rd edition. London: Routledge Kegan Paul.

HM Government (2003) *Every child matters: Change for children*. **www.everychildmatters.gov.uk**

Høiskar, AH (2001) Under age and under fire: An inquiry into the use of child soldiers, 1994–98. *Childhood*, 2001 (8): 340–60.

Hokenstad, M and Midgley, J (eds) (1997) *Issues in international social work*. Washington, DC: NASW Press.

Home Office (2008) *Asylum statistics: 1st quarter 2008 United Kingdom.* **www.homeoffice.gov.uk**

Hopton, J (2006) The future of critical psychiatry. *Critical Social Policy*, 26(1): 57–73.

Hreinsdóttir, E E, Stefánsdóttir, G, Lewthwaite, A, Ledger, S and Shufflebotham, L (2006) Is my story so different from yours? Comparing life stories, experiences of institutionalisation and self-advocacy in England and Iceland. *British Journal of Learning Disabilities*, 34(3): 157–66.

Huegler, N (2005) *Care and support for young separated refugees aged 16 and 17 in Germany and the United Kingdom*. Birmingham: Venture Press.

Hugman, R (1994) *Ageing and the care of older people in Europe*. Basingstoke: Macmillan.

Hugman, R (2007) The place of values in social work education. In Lymbery, M and Postle, K (eds) *Social work: A companion to learning*. London: Sage.

Humphries, M (1996) *Empty cradles*. London: Corgi Adult.

Humphries, S and Gordon, P (1992) *Out of sight: The experience of disability 1900–1950*. Plymouth: Northcote House Publishers.

Innocenti Research Centre (2007) *Report card 7: Child poverty in perspective: An overview of child well-being in rich countries – a comprehensive assessment of the lives and well-being of children and adolescents in the economically advanced nations*. Florence: United Nations Children's Fund (UNICEF).

International Association of Schools of Social Work (IASSW) (2005) *Global standards for social work education and training for social work professions.* **www.iassw-aiets.org/**

International Federation of Social Workers (IFSW) (2000) *Definition of social work.* **www.ifsw.org**

International Federation of Social Workers (IFSW) (2004) *Ethics in social work, statement of principles.* **www.ifsw.org**

International Labour Organization (2006) *Facts on child labour – 2006*. **www.ilo.org**

International Labour Organization (2007) *Equality at work: Tackling the challenges. Global report under the follow-up to the ILO Declaration on fundamental principles and rights at work.* **www.ilo.org**

International Social Services UK (ISS UK) (2008) **www.issuk.org.uk**

Islam, Z (2008) Negotiating identities: The lives of Pakistani and Bangladeshi young disabled people. *Disability and Society*, 23 (1): 41–52.

Jacoby, R (1999) *The end of Utopia: Politics and culture in an age of apathy.* New York: Basic Books.

Kale, R (1995) South Africa's health: Traditional healers in South Africa: A parallel health care system. *British Medical Journal*, 3(10): 1182–85.

Kendall, K. (2000) *Social work education: Its origins in Europe*. Alexandria, VA: Council on Social Work Education.

Kim, KM (2008) The current status and future of centers for independent living in Korea. *Disability and Society,* 23(1): 67–76.

Kohli, R (2006) The sound of silence: Listening to what unaccompanied asylum-seeking children say and do not say. *British Journal of Social Work*, 36: 707–21.

Kohli, R and Mather, R (2003) Promoting psychosocial well-being in unaccompanied asylum seeking young people in the United Kingdom. *Child and Family Social Work,* (8): 201–12.

Kokai, M, Fujii, S, Shinfuku, N and Edwards, G (2004) Natural disaster and mental health in Asia. *Psychiatry and Clinical Neurosciences*, 58(2): 110–16.

Laing, RD (1967) *The politics of experience and the bird of paradise*. Harmondsworth: Penguin.

Laming, H (2003) The Victoria Climbié Inquiry. **www.victoria-climbie-inquiry.org.uk**

Lavalette, M, and Ferguson I (eds) (2007) *International social work and the radical tradition*. Birmingham: Venture Press.

Lewis, P (2007) The sorry plight of the refugee children. *The Guardian*, 24 May 2007.

Littlechild, B, Erath, P and Keller, J (eds) (2005) *De- and reconstruction in European social work*. Stassfurt: ISIS.

Lorenz, W (1994) *Social work in a changing Europe*. London: Routledge.

Lucock, B, Lefevre, M, Orr, D, Jones, M, Marchant, R and Tanner, K (2006) *Teaching, learning and assessing communication skills with children and young people in social work education*. Social work education knowledge review 12. Social Care Institute for Excellence. **www.scie.org.uk**

Lymbery, M (2005) *Social work with older people*. London: Sage.

Lyons K (1999) *International social work: Themes and perspectives*. Aldershot: Ashgate.

Lyons, K (2003) Historical portraits: Dame Eileen Younghusband (Jan 1902 – May 1981). *Social Work and Society*, 1. **www.socwork.net**

Lyons, K and Lawrence, S (eds) (2006) *Social work in Europe: Educating for change*. Birmingham: IASSW/Venture Press.

Lyons, K and Littlechild, B (eds) (2006) *International labour mobility in social work*. BASW Monograph. Birmingham: Venture Press.

Lyons, K and Manion, HK (2004) Goodbye DipSW: Trends in student satisfaction and employment outcomes. *Social Work Education*, 23(2): 133–48.

Lyons, K and Stathopoulos, P (2001) Migration and refugees in Europe: Greek and British perspectives on implications for social work practice and education. *European Journal of Social Work*, 4(1): 55–63.

Lyons, K, Manion, K and Carlsen, M (2006) *International perspectives on social work.* Basingstoke: Palgrave Macmillan.

Macpherson, W (1999) The Stephen Lawrence Inquiry. **www.archive.official-documents.co.uk**

Maiello, S (2008) Encounter with a traditional healer: Western and African therapeutic approaches in dialogue. *Journal of Analytical Psychology,* 53 (2): 241–60.

Maslow, AH (1954) *Motivation and personality.* 2nd edition. New York: Harper and Row Publishers.

Meeuwisse, A and Sward, H (2007) Cross-national comparisons of social work – a question of initial assumptions and levels of analysis. *European Journal of Social Work*, 10(4): 481–96.

Mental Health Act Commission (2008) *Annual Report.* London: The Stationery Office.

Mental Health Foundation (2004) *Black and minority ethnic communities and mental health.* **www.mhf.org.uk**

Merton, R (1957) *Social theory and social structure.* New York: Free Press.

Mind (2006) The mental health of the African Caribbean community in Britain. **www.mind.org.uk**

Mitchell, D, Traustadottir, R, Chapman, R, Townson, L, Ingham N and Ledger, S (2006) *Exploring experiences of advocacy by people with learning disabilities: Testimonies of resistance.* London: Jessica Kingsley Press.

Morris, J (1991) *Pride against prejudice: Transforming attitudes to disability.* London: The Women's Press.

Morris, S (2007) Murder victim was failed by the system. *The Guardian*, 6 December 2007. **www.guardian.co.uk**

Muncie, J (1999) *Youth and crime: A critical introduction.* London: Sage.

Munday, B (2007) *Integrated social services in Europe.* Strasbourg: Council of Europe Publishing.

Mupedziswa, R (2001) The quest for relevance: Towards a conceptual model of developmental social work education and training in Africa. *International Social Work,* 44 (3): 285–300.

National Alliance on Mental Illness Santa Cruz County (2005) *Mental health recovery: What helps and what hinders?* **www.namiscc.org**

Nirje, B (1969) The normalisation principle and its human management implications. In Kugel, RB and Wolfensberger, W (eds) *Changing patterns in residential services for the mentally retarded.* Washington, DC: US Government Printing Office. An abridged version can be accessed at: **www.socialrolevalorization.com**

Njenga, FG, Nicholls, PJ, Nyamai, C, Kigamwa, P and Davidson, JRT (2004) Post-traumatic stress after terrorist attack: Psychological reactions following the US embassy bombing in Nairobi: Naturalistic study. *British Journal of Psychiatry,* 185(4): 328–33.

North, CS, Pfefferbaum, B, Narayanan, P, Thielman, S, McCoy, G, Dumont, C-K, Aya-Ryosho, N and Spitznagel, EL (2005) Comparison of post-disaster psychiatric disorders after terrorist bombings in Nairobi and Oklahoma City. *British Journal of Psychiatry*, 186(6): 487–93.

Norward, JN (2007) Social work and social activism in post-democratic South Africa. In Lavalette, M and Ferguson, I (eds) *International social work and the radical tradition*. Birmingham: Venture Press/BASW/IASSW.

Office for National Statistics (2004) *Pupils with statements of Special Educational Needs (SEN): by type of school. Data set 34.* **www.statistics.gov.uk**

Office for National Statistics (2005) *Focus on older people.* **www.statistics.gov.uk**

Office for the United Nations High Commission for Human Rights (2006) *Optional Protocol to the Convention against Torture and other Cruel, Inhuman or Degrading Treatment or Punishment.* **www2.ohchr.org**

O'Hagan, K (1999) Culture, cultural identity and cultural sensitivity in child and family social work. *Child and Family Social Work*, 4(4): 269–81.

Oliver, M (1990) *The politics of disablement*. London: Macmillan.

Oliver, M (1999) Capitalism, disability and ideology: A materialist critique of the normalisation principle. In Flyn, R and Lemay, R (eds) *A quarter-century of normalization and social role valorization: Evaluation and impact*. Ottawa: University of Ottawa Press.

Palmer, G (2007) *Disabled people, poverty and the labour market. Updated report.* **www.poverty.org.uk**

Palmer, G, Carr, J and Kenway, P (2005) *Monitoring poverty and social exclusion*. York: Joseph Rowntree Foundation. (The report can be accessed in PDF format at **www.npi.org.uk**

Papadopoulos, RK (ed) (2002) *Therapeutic care for refugees. No place like home*. London: Karnac.

Parekh Report (2000) *The future of multi-ethnic Britain*. London: Profile Books.

Parker, J and Bradley, G (2007) *Social work practice: Assessment, planning, intervention and review.* 2nd edition. Exeter: Learning Matters.

Parker, R (2007) *Uprooted: The shipment of poor children to Canada, 1867–1917*. Bristol: Policy Press.

Parkes, CM, Laungani, P and Young, B (1997) *Death and bereavement across cultures*. London: Routledge.

Payne, M (2005) *The origins of social work: Continuity and change*. Basingstoke: Palgrave Macmillan.

Pease, B and Pringle, K (eds) (2001) *A man's world? Changing men's practices in a globalised world*. London: Zed Books.

Petrie, P, Boddy, J, Cameron, C, Wigfall, V and Simon, A (2006) *Working with children in care: European perspectives*. Maidenhead: Open University Press.

Phillips, J, Ray, M and Marshall, M (2006) *Social work with older people*. Basingstoke: Palgrave Macmillan.

Philpott, J (2007) Britain's Eastern European migrant workforce. *Impact*, Issue 19: 24–27.

Pilgrim, D and Rogers, A (1999) *A sociology of mental health and illness.* 2nd edition. Buckingham: Open University Press.

Price, V (2008) *A European approach to day care for learning disabled people: Spot the difference?* Unpublished paper. University of Wolverhampton.

Price, V and Simpson, G (2007) *Transforming society? Social work and sociology.* Bristol: Policy Press.

Pringle, K (1998) *Children and social welfare in Europe.* Buckingham: Open University Press.

Quality Assurance Agency (2008) *Subject benchmark statement: Social work.* QAA 236 02/08.**http://www.qaa.ac.uk**

Race, D (2007) *Intellectual disability: Social approaches.* Maidenhead: McGraw-Hill Open University Press.

Race, D (ed) (2003) *Leadership and change in human services: Selected readings from Wolf Wolfensberger.* London: Routledge.

Race, D, Boxhall, K and Carson, I (2005) Towards a dialogue for practice: Reconciling social role valorization and the social model of disability. *Disability and Society,* 20(5): 507–21.

Ratha, D, Mohapatra, S, Vijayalakshmi, KM and Xu, Zhimei (2008) *Revisions to remittance trends 2007.* **http://siteresources.worldbank.org**

Rethink (2004) *Recovery: A brief introduction to the recovery approach.* **www.rethink.org**

Rethink (2007) *Who does it affect?* **www.rethink.org**

Richman, N. (1998) *In the midst of a whirlwind: A manual for helping refugee children.* Stoke-on-Trent: Trentham Books/Save the Children.

Ritzer, G (1993) *The McDonaldisation of society.* Thousand Oaks, CA: Pine Forge Press.

Roberts, K and Harris, J (2002) *Disabled people in refugee and asylum seeking communities.* Bristol: Policy Press and Joseph Rowntree Foundation.

Rolph, S, Atkinson, D and Walmsey, J (2003) A pair of stout shoes and an umbrella: The role of the mental welfare officer in delivering community care in East Anglia: 1946–1970. *British Journal of Social Work*, 33(3): 339–59.

Rolph, S, Atkinson, D, Nind, M and Welshman, J (2005) *Witnesses to change: Families, history and learning disability.* London: British Institute of Learning Disabilities.

Ross, S and Brown, C (2006) Scottish staff stunned by Norwich Union job cuts. *The Scotsman Business*, 15 September 2006. **http://business.scotsman.com**

Rot, A (2007) Disability in the Netherlands. Unpublished briefing. HS in Holland, Amsterdam.

Sanders, M (2003) Working with interpreters in personal social services. In Kornbeck, J (ed) *Language teaching in social work education.* Mainz: Logophone.

Schädler, J, Schwarte, N, Wissel,T and Aselmeier, L (2004) Research feature: Germany. *Tizard Learning Disability Review,* 9(1).

Scottish Disability Equality Forum (SDEF) (2007) *Written response to the Scottish Government budget, 2007.* **www.scottish.parliament.uk**

Scull, A (1977) *Decarceration: Community treatment and the deviant – a radical view*. Englewood Cliffs, NJ: Prentice Hall.

Scull, A (1983) Community corrections: Panacea, progress or pretence? In Garland, D and Young, P (eds) *The power to punish*. London: Heinemann.

Seebohm, P (2008) *Briefing 35: Evening the odds: Employment support, mental health and Black and minority ethnic communities*. London: Sainsbury Centre for Mental Health. (Online version available at: **www.scmh.org.uk**

Sefton, T, Baker, M and Praat, A (2006) *Ethnic minorities, disability and a review of the labour market. Ethnicity, disability and work project*. Royal National Institute for the Blind. **www.rnib.org.uk**

Seibel, FW and Lorenz, W (eds) (1998) *Social professions for a social Europe: Conference on the evaluation of the ERASMUS Programme in Koblenz (Germany) 5–7 July 1996*. Frankfurt/M: IKO.

Shakespeare, T (2006) *Disability rights and wrongs*. London: Routledge.

Sheppard, M, Newstead, S, DiCaccavo, A and Ryan, K (2001) Comparative hypothesis assessment and quasi triangulation as process knowledge assessment strategies in social work practice. *British Journal of Social Work*, 31(6): 863–85.

Social Care Institute for Excellence (SCIE) (2006) *Social Care Code of Practice for International Recruitment*. **www.sccir.org.uk**

Sozialgesetzbuch IX (2001) **www.sozialgesetzbuch-bundessozialhilfegesetz.de**

Special pedagogiska skol myndigheten (SPSM) (2008) National Agency for Special Needs Education and Schools. **www.spsm.se**

Sriskandarajah, D and Drew, C (2006) *Brits abroad: Mapping the scale and nature of British emigration*. London: Institute for Public Policy Research.

Statistics Norway (2007) *Adoptions, by type of adoption 1966–2006*. **www.ssb.no/english**

Swain, J, Finkelstein, V, French, S and Oliver, M (eds) (1993) *Disabling barriers – enabling environments*. London: Sage.

Szasz, T (1971) *The manufacture of madness*. London: Routledge and Kegan Paul.

Tew, J and Foster, J (2005) *Social perspectives in mental health*. London: Jessica Kingsley Publishers.

The Guardian (2007) Chad accuses French charity of child trafficking. 29 October 2007. **www.guardian.co.uk**

The Guardian (2008) Feeling the squeeze: As the economy tips into recession and public spending takes a hit, will the axe fall on health and welfare services that protect the most vulnerable people? A panel of experts give their views on the potential fallout. Society Guardian, 22 October 2008.

The Scotsman Business (2006) BT to hire 6,000 in Indian expansion. 14 November 2006. **http://business.scotsman.com**

Thomas, P (2005) *Disability, poverty and the millennium development goals: Relevance, challenges and opportunities for DFID*. Knowledge and Research Programme.

Torres, S (2006) Making sense of the construct of successful ageing. In Daatland, S and Biggs, S (eds) *Ageing and diversity*. Bristol: Policy Press.

Tribe, R and Raval, H (ed) (2002) *Working with interpreters in mental health*. London: Brummer-Routledge.

Turning Point (2004) *Hidden lives*. London: Turning Point.

UNICEF (2007a) Paris Conference, *'Free Children from War'*. **www.unicef.org**

UNICEF (2007b) adapted. **www.unicef.org.uk/campaigns**

UNICEF (2009) *Russian Federation: Statistics*. **www.unicef.org**

United Nations (2007) *World population ageing 2007*. **www.un.org**

United Nations (2008) *United Nations convention on the rights of persons with disabilities*. **www.un.org**

United Nations convention and protocol relating to the status of refugees (1951). **www.unhcr.org**

United Nations convention on the rights of the child (UNCRC) (1989). **www.unicef.org/crc/**

United Nations Educational, Scientific and Cultural Organisation (UNESCO) (2007) *Education for all: Global monitoring report (summary)*. Paris: EFA Global Monitoring Report Team.

United Nations Population Fund (UNFPA) (2007) *The state of world population 2007: Unleashing the potential of urban growth*. **www.unfpa.org**

US Census Bureau (2009) *International data base*. **www.census.gov**

Van Dyk,, A (2001) *Western and African mental health. Paper presented at the European Congress of Psychology, 4 July, London. Press release accessible at* **www.bps.org.uk**

Vlaskamp, C and Poppes, P (2004) Research feature: The Netherlands. *Tizard Learning Disability Review* 9(1).

Walker, A and Maltby, T (1997) *Ageing Europe*. Buckingham: Open University Press.

Walls, P and Sashidharan, SP (2003) *Real voices – survey findings from a series of community consultation events involving Black and Minority Ethnic groups in England*. London: Department of Health.

Warnes, AM and Williams, A (2006) Older migrants in Europe: A new focus for migration studies. *Journal of Ethnic and Migration Studies*, 32(8): 1257–81.

Warnes, AM, Friedrich, K, Kellaher, L and Torres, S (2004) The diversity and welfare of older migrants in Europe. *Ageing and Society*, 24(3): 307–26.

Warnes, T (2006) Older foreign migrants in Europe: Multiple pathways and welfare positions. In Daatland, S and Biggs, S (eds) *Ageing and diversity*. Bristol: Policy Press.

Weiss, I (2005) Is there a global common core to social work? A cross-national comparative study on the professional ideology of social work graduates. *Social Work*, 50(2): 101–10.

Welbourne, P, Harrison, G and Ford, D (2007) Social work in the UK and the global labour market. *International Social Work*, 50(1): 27–40.

Winkelmann-Gleed, A (2006) *Migrant nurses: Motivation, integration and contribution*. Abingdon: Radcliffe Publishing.

Women's Commission for Refugee Women and Children (2008) *Disabilities among refugees and conflict-affected populations.* **www.womenscommission.org**

World Health Organisation (2001) *The world health report 2001 – Mental health: New understanding, new hope.* **www.who.int**

World Health Organisation (2005) *The Tsunami and After: WHO's role.* WHO Regional Office for South-East Asia. **www.searo.who.int**

World Health Organisation (2006) *Disability and rehabilitation: WHO action plan 2006–2011.* **www.who.int**

World Health Organisation (2007a) *Mental health: A state of well-being.* **www.who.int**

World Health Organisation (2007b) *Breaking the vicious cycle between mental ill-health and poverty.* Geneva: World Health Organisation.

World Health Organisation (2007c) WHO *celebrates International Day of Persons with Disabilities* **www.who.int**

World Health Organisation (2008a) *Policies and practices for mental health in Europe – meeting the challenges.* Copenhagen: WHO Regional Office for Europe.

World Health Organisation (2008b) *Country information.* **www.who.int**

World Health Organisation (2008c) **www.who.int**

Yeo, R (2005) *Disability, poverty and the new development agenda.* **www.disabilitykar.net**

Zack-Williams, AB (2006) Child soldiers in Sierra Leone and the problems of demobilization, rehabilitation and reintegration into society: Some lessons for social workers in war-torn societies. *Social Work Education*, 25 (2): 119–28.

Index

interpreters, working through 41–3
Inter-University Centre Dubrovnik (IUC) 117
Islam, funeral arrangements 82
Islam, Zoebia 98

Jebb, Eglantyne 111
journeys 9–10

Korea, independent living in 104

labour migrants 80
Laming, Lord 48, 58
Law 180 (Italy) 73
learning disabilities 96–76, 106–7
  employment prospects and 100–2
life changes 68, 81–4
  transition and loss 81–2
life expectancy 78
Local Authority Social Services Act 1970 109
lone-parent families 39
Loomis, Ray 106
loss, dealing with 81–2

marital breakdown 40
Marxist conflict theories of crime 17
Maslow's hierarchy of needs 47
mass movement of people 5, 9–10 see also
    migration
McDonaldisation of society 23–4
membership of international associations
    114–15
mental ill health 60–75
  in BME groups 69–71
  causes of 65–8
  definitions of 61–2
  different world views 63–4
  global perspectives 62–3
  policy 72–4
  potential sufferers 64–5
  social models 64
Merton's theoretical approach 17
micro-credit 103
migrants
  integration between generations 56
  low paid employment 19, 102
migration 19–22
  impact on old age 79–81
  see also diaspora
minimum wage 53
mobile phones 22, 23
mourning 81–2
  socially constructed 81
movement of capital 16–19
Muslims see Islam

National Assistance Act 1948 109
National Conference of Social Work 112
National Society for the Prevention of Cruelty to
    Children (NSPCC) 111
Nationality, Immigration and Asylum Act 2002
  assisted return under 80–1

Nazi movement 36
Netherlands, independent living in 105
Nirje, Bengt 96–7
non-governmental organisations (NGOs) 36, 37
  definitions of disbility 94
  home care provision by 87
normalisation movement 96–7
Norway 106–7
nurses, as labour migrants 80

older people see elders
Oliver, Michael 95, 96, 97
overseas aid pledges 17

Parma
  disabled training and employment 101
  home care in 87
Patients' Councils, origins of 3
pensions 86
People First movement 106
people smuggling 21
people trafficking 21–2
personalisation agenda 93, 104
Poor Law 1834 109
post-traumatic stress disorder (PTSD) 65, 66
  elder migrants with 81
poverty
  and BME groups 19, 55
  and child soldiers 50
  and disability 95, 102–4
  and elders 86
  factors associated with 18
  relationship with mental ill health 67–8
private sector agencies 35–6

Race, David 97, 106–7
recovery approach 71, 74
recruitment 117–18
Red Crescent 5, 111
Red Cross 5, 9, 111
refugees 20
  children 49–52
  with disabilities 102
rehabilitation
  community-based approach to in Africa 50
  disabled people 105
relocation of jobs 17–18, 22
remittances 17
residential care 89
return migrants 80–1
rights, children's 47–8
Ritzer, George 23–4
Russia, life expectancy in 78
Rwanda, poverty and disability in 103

Salomon, Alice 110, 112
Sand, Dr René 112
Save the Children 111
Scottish Disability Equality Forum (SDEF) 97
self-advocacy 98, 106, 107
self-help groups 64